A
SHAKESPEARE MANUAL
FOR SCHOOLS

A
SHAKESPEARE MANUAL
FOR SCHOOLS

BY

W. A. ILLSLEY, M.A.
Government College, Zaria, N. Nigeria

CAMBRIDGE
AT THE UNIVERSITY PRESS
1957

CAMBRIDGE
UNIVERSITY PRESS

University Printing House, Cambridge CB2 8BS, United Kingdom

Cambridge University Press is part of the University of Cambridge.

It furthers the University's mission by disseminating knowledge in the pursuit of
education, learning and research at the highest international levels of excellence.

www.cambridge.org
Information on this title: www.cambridge.org/9781107544574

First published 1957
First paperback edition 2015

A catalogue record for this publication is available from the British Library

ISBN 978-1-107-54457-4 Paperback

CONTENTS

ILLUSTRATIONS

PREFACE

Several years' experience of introducing the study of Shakespeare's plays to Nigerian students in a Government secondary school has convinced me that the need exists for a book which can guide the pupil clearly and simply through his early difficulties to enjoyment and appreciation of the plays.

None of the annotated editions of the plays is wholly satisfactory to the student studying Shakespeare for the first time, unless the guidance of a specialist teacher is available, to supplement notes where necessary, to explain technicalities, and to advise which details are trivial and which important. In West Africa, and in many other oversea territories where educational programmes are developing swiftly, there is a shortage of specialist teachers; and this book is intended primarily for use as a class-book to help both pupils, and teachers who have no qualifications in English literature, in their study of Shakespeare. It is hoped that in Great Britain, also, the book will be found helpful to many students studying the plays, without a specialist to guide them.

The second part of the book deals frankly with the problem how the student may use, to the best advantage, in written examinations, his acquired knowledge and understanding of the plays. There is no reason why the proper study of a book or play for an examination should mar or diminish the enjoyment of the student of that particular text. Throughout this manual, illustrative quotations have been taken, where possible, from the plays most frequently set for the School Certificate examinations; and there is a section consisting of examination questions on six selected plays, which busy teachers, and students preparing externally for examinations, may find useful.

The lines in all textual references are numbered according to the Oxford Edition of Shakespeare's Works, published in 1904, and edited by W. J. Craig.

W. A. I.

ZARIA
28 August 1956

The Plays

SHAKESPEARE'S PLAYS

Shakespeare was born in 1564 and died in 1616, and there is general agreement among scholars that his working life lasted from 1590 to 1613, during which time he wrote the thirty-seven plays usually acknowledged as his. There is some doubt as to which plays he wrote, owing to the fact that they were not collected until 1623, when two of his friends, John Heming and Henry Condell, published the 'First Folio', which claimed his authorship for thirty-six plays: *Pericles* was added later. During Shakespeare's lifetime some of his plays had been published, but it is uncertain whether any of these were printed by his consent, and some of them were, doubtless, 'pirated' editions, shortened or garbled versions sold off to the publisher by the actors' companies (which owned the plays) to make money in bad times.

Even Shakespeare's authorship has been disputed, as parts of his life are still in shadow, and arguments have been advanced on behalf of Lord Bacon, the Earls of Oxford, Derby and Rutland, and, more recently, Christopher Marlowe has gained fresh support. In spite of spirited controversy, the evidence, tradition, and the opinion of the majority of scholars, leave Shakespeare's position as firm as ever.

With the possible exception of one early play (*Love's Labour's Lost*), and one late play (*The Tempest*), Shakespeare's plots are not original. He derived his material from many sources, from classical and historical plays and stories. The two books to which he was most indebted are North's *Plutarch's Lives* from which he obtained the plots of his Roman plays (for example, the lives of Coriolanus, Caesar and Antonius), and Holinshed's *Chronicle*, from which he borrowed the material for his plays on English history. It was quite usual for writers for the Elizabethan stage to borrow in this way, and Shakespeare need not be accused of mere copying or plagiarism. If you compare his source-material with his finished plays, you will agree that what he borrowed he made his own, and that his dramatic and literary skill changed what was lead to gold.

The plays are divided into three main groups, the Tragedies, Histories and Comedies. Briefly, a tragedy is a play with an ending in which the hero, or main character, is overcome by the forces which have been gathering round him, and perishes, because of some defect in his character. Its effect is to warn us, to move us to pity, that Man can thus be overwhelmed. *Macbeth*, or *Julius Caesar*, are typical. An historical play deals with part of the life and reign of one of the British kings, such as *Henry V*. A comedy is not merely an amusing play, but one in which the hero proves superior to circumstances, and therefore his destiny is fortunate, and the play has a happy ending. Some scholars would subdivide this classification: for instance, although *The Merchant of Venice* is generally classed as a comedy, the unhappy fate of Shylock is a discordant element to a true comedy, and they would argue that it should not be included as such.

The Reading List on p. 86 gives the titles of books dealing in greater detail with all the subjects touched on above, for those whose interest, or course of study, requires them to do further reading.

ACTS, SCENES AND PLAYERS

If you have never studied one of Shakespeare's plays before, several things will appear strange to you when you turn to the first page of the text. The lines of printing do not extend from edge to edge of the page: in fact, you might correctly assume that the play was written in some form of verse, as poetry is. Although the pages are numbered, you cannot find any chapter divisions. Some of the printing is in italic. These things are confusing until you know the reason for them.

When you look at the first page of a play, in addition to what has been mentioned above, you notice the words 'Act' and 'Scene'. In *Henry V* they appear in this way:

Act I.

Scene i. London. An Antechamber in the King's Palace.

Let us consider an 'Act' first. This is the name given to a major division of a play. To perform a lengthy play without any pause or rest would require an impossible effort by both actors and audience, so the Acts serve to provide an interval for relaxation. In theory, there may be any number of them in a play; Shakespeare prefers five. An Act, however, is not a separate part of the play; each Act is connected to its fellow by the continuous story, and tells the story to a point at which it is convenient to pause. If we gave briefly the sections of the story of the play *Henry V* as they appear in the five Acts, our summary would be like this:

Act I. Reasons for the invasion of France by King Henry.
Act II. Preparations for the invasion.
Act III. Early successes in the campaign.
Act IV. Agincourt.
Act V. The peace settlement and conclusion of the play.

Each Act is sub-divided into a number of *Scenes*. Some Acts may contain as many as seven scenes; others, as few as two. A scene may be defined as that portion of an Act which is performed without change of place. For instance, in the example given from *Henry V*, Scene i reads:

London. An Antechamber in the King's Palace.

Scene ii is:

The Same. The Presence Chamber.

By 'The Same', it is indicated that the action is still taking place in the King's Palace in London, but, as you can see from what follows, in a different room.

Occasionally there is an exception to the definition. It sometimes happens that the place of the action does not change, although a new scene begins. For example, in *Macbeth*, Act I, Scene i is 'Inverness. Court within the Castle'. At the beginning of Scene ii we read:

Scene ii. *The Same.*

Here, as you can see by reference to the play, the actors have changed even though the place has not; and therefore a new scene was begun.

We are not sure that the division into Acts and scenes always follows Shakespeare's original plan, since much of it was completed at a later date (1709) by Nicholas Rowe.

In each scene you will notice that the lines are numbered. This is for convenience of reference. You do not refer to page numbers as you would in a book, but to the Act, scene and line, when you wish to give a reference in a play:

Through tatter'd clothes small vices do appear.
King Lear, Act IV, scene vi, line 169.

An abbreviation which you will come across in this connection is ll., which is short for 'lines'. A single l. is frequently used for 'line', and scene is abbreviated to 'sc.' This method of reference is essential, unless everyone is using the same text, because in different texts the page numbering is different, and an attempt to give references by means of the page numbers would soon lead to confusion.

While you have been looking through the text you will have noticed that, in addition to the speaker's name being printed in italic at the beginning of each speech, there are instructions printed in italic, and often enclosed in square brackets, occurring in some of the scenes. Here is an example from *Richard II*:

> *Queen.* ...   .
> My wretchedness unto a row of pins,
> They'll talk of state; for everyone doth so
> Against a change: woe is forerun with woe.
>
> *[Queen and Ladies retire.*
> *Enter a Gardener and two Servants.*[1]

The words printed in italic are called Stage Directions, and are simply the instructions given by the writer of the play to the actors and the producer of the play to help them in understanding how he wishes the play to be performed. Shakespeare did not write very full stage directions; if you look at some modern plays—those by Bernard Shaw, for instance—you will see how much more detailed the stage directions are.

In most cases, the directions explain themselves; but a number of terms, which appear frequently, and may not be understood, are explained below:

Exit. He (she) goes out.

Exeunt. They go out.

Aside. The speech which this term qualifies is intended to be spoken so that the audience may hear it, but not the other characters on the stage unless the direction indicates that the speaker is addressing another person in the aside. You must imagine that the actor speaking the aside is voicing his secret thoughts.

Alarums, Excursions. Noises, such as the blowing of trumpets, and the entry and exit of parties of soldiers on the stage, usually to give the impression that a battle is taking place.

Flourish. Blowing of trumpets such as would take place before the entry of a noble person, or before some important announcement.

[1] *Rich. II*, III, iv, 26–8.

13

Swoons. Faints, becomes unconscious.

Starts. Gives a sudden movement, as of surprise or fear.

Talk apart. Two or more of the persons on the stage talk separately from the remaining people, and are not heard by the audience.

Within. From an unseen room within the building which is being represented on the stage. (See also the chapter on the Elizabethan Theatre and Stage.)

Without. Outside the building or room which is being represented on the stage.

Above, aloft. On the balcony above the stage, or in the loft still higher above the stage, in the Elizabethan theatre.

Below, beneath. Underneath the stage.

DRAMATIS PERSONAE

These words mean 'the people of the play', and you will find them at the beginning of the play, printed above a list of the names of all the people who are to take part in that play. There are two ways of compiling such a list: the names may be set down in order of seniority, with the male characters coming first, or they may be set down according to the order in which the characters appear on the stage. Shakespeare prefers the former method. First all the male characters are listed, in order of seniority, and then all the female characters, also in order of seniority. After these comes a list of those persons also required for crowd scenes and the like: the people who are known as 'extras', in the language of the cinema. In this list will come such people as lords, ladies, officers, soldiers, citizens, messengers, and attendants. (That list, slightly altered, is to be found at the beginning of *Henry V.*)

PROLOGUE

A Prologue is an introductory speech, and in Shakespeare's plays it takes the form of verses spoken by a Chorus (*Henry V*), by a person who represents the Prologue (*Henry VIII*) or by someone representing Rumour (*Henry IV, Part II*). These introductions are particularly valuable before an historical play, as they enable the author to explain to the audience the events which have preceded the commencement of the play, or to give an outline of the main happenings which will take place in the course of the play.

This is a short speech intended to round off the play. Frequently it asks quite openly for applause for the play which has just been performed, and it may also indicate what the author intends to write about in the future. At the end of *Henry IV, Part II*, the Epilogue, spoken by a Dancer, says:

...I was lately here in the end of a displeasing play, to pray your patience for it and to promise you a better.[1]

Prospero, speaking the Epilogue at the end of *The Tempest* asks the audience to

> ...release me from my bands
> With the help of your good hands,[2]

that is to say, by clapping.

THE STRUCTURE OF THE PLAYS

SCENE ANALYSIS

The opening scene. In any play, the opening scene is of great importance, as it sets the tone for what is to follow. A weak opening gives the audience a bad impression, which the rest of the play may never completely erase. The playwright wishes his opening scene:

(*a*) To be dramatically effective. It may surprise, startle or amuse the audience, thus gaining their immediate attention.

(*b*) To set the tone of the play. The audience must be given an idea what the purpose of the play is.

[1] *Henry IV, Part II*, Epilogue, ll. 9–12.
[2] *The Tempest*, Epilogue, ll. 9–10.

(*c*) To introduce the main plot, give vital information, and make the audience wish for more.

Shakespeare constructs his opening scenes to carry out all these functions. He had, in addition, to overcome a problem which is not often met by modern playwrights, that of noise in the audience. At the beginning of a play in the Elizabethan theatre, there was probably a considerable tumult going on among the audience, particularly among the 'groundlings', as those who stood in the pit (the cheapest part of the theatre), were called. From contemporary accounts, we know that all sorts of bad characters mingled with the onlookers—pickpockets, gamblers and ruffians—and that there was frequently quarrelling and shouting.[1] Shakespeare's opening scenes had to be dramatic enough to seize the attention of this somewhat disorderly company, and make it listen, after the signal had been given by three trumpet blasts, that the play was about to begin.

The length of the opening scenes varies considerably; *Macbeth*, for instance, has a first scene of twelve lines, and *Richard II* one of two hundred and five. Each, however, fulfils its author's purposes, though in different ways, as can be seen from consideration of the points given above:

(*a*) *Macbeth*. The scene is dramatically effective by reason of the noise of thunder and the storm, and the horrifying appearance of the three witches, which would startle a superstitious Elizabethan audience.

Richard II. The entrance of the King and his attendant nobles, with full ceremonial, makes an impressive opening.

(*b*) *Macbeth*. The tone is at once set by the words of the three witches—'Fair is foul, and foul is fair.'[2] The play will be concerned with a reversal of the natural order of things, and dominated by supernatural powers.

---

[1] 'These are the youths that thunder at a playhouse, and fight for bitten apples.' (Porter, *Henry VIII*, v, iv, 65–6.)

[2] *Macbeth*, I, i, 11.

Richard II. We see that there is dissension in the king-dom, and bitter hatred between two over-mighty subjects, Bolingbroke and Mowbray, which the King is powerless to control.

(*c*) *Macbeth.* From the twelve short lines, we learn that a battle is proceeding, which will end before sunset, and that after the battle the witches will reassemble to meet Macbeth on the heath.

Richard II. Bolingbroke, son of John of Gaunt, and cousin of Richard, has accused Mowbray of the murder of the Duke of Gloucester, and other offences, and the King orders trial by combat to decide the issue, after attempts at reconciliation have failed.

It can be seen that each opening would have instant appeal to the audience, and reveal sufficient of the plot to excite interest and impatience for what was to follow. Sometimes the appeal is made to the eye, sometimes to the ear: occasionally, Rumour or a Prologue introduces the first scene. You should study for yourselves the opening scenes of other Shakespearean plays, on the lines suggested, noting how the impact is made, and trying to imagine how they would sound and look upon the stage. The opening scene of *Hamlet* is a good example to take, for it has all the qualities necessary for success—atmo-sphere, drama, the supernatural, speeches of high quality, and mystery.

Later Scenes. On looking through some of the plays, you may be puzzled about the reason for the inclusion of certain scenes, particularly if they are very short ones, of only a few lines. A more careful examination of the scene may provide the reason, and it will be found that the scene, at first sight superfluous, advances our understanding of either plot or character, or both.

Here is a short scene from *As You Like It* (Act II, sc. vi), which may not immediately appear to be very important, but which has a necessary part in the play:

Scene vi. *Another part of the Forest*

Enter ORLANDO *and* ADAM

Adam. Dear master, I can go no further: O! I die for food. Here I lie down, and measure out my grave. Farewell, kind master.

Orl. Why, how now, Adam! no greater heart in thee? Live a little; comfort a little; cheer thyself a little. If this uncouth forest yield anything savage, I will either be food for it, or bring it for food to thee. Thy conceit is nearer death than thy powers. For my sake be comfortable, hold death awhile at the arm's end, I will here be with thee presently, and if I bring thee not something to eat, I will give thee leave to die; but if thou diest before I come, thou art a mocker of my labour. Well said! thou lookest cheerly, and I'll be with thee quickly. Yet thou liest in the bleak air: come I will bear thee to some shelter, and thou shalt not die for lack of a dinner, if there live anything in this desert. Cheerly, good Adam. [*Exeunt*

When we come to study this scene more closely, we observe the following things:

1. *Character.* *Adam* is shown to be so loyal to his master that he has followed him, without complaint, almost to death. Even in this extremity, he refers to Orlando as 'dear', and 'kind'.

Orlando's bravery, tenderness and thoughtfulness are brought out here. He declares himself willing to sacrifice his own life to bring food for Adam. He speaks to the old man gently and kindly, and tries to cheer him up with a little joke. Before he goes off on his search, he remembers that Adam is exposed to the cold, and carries him carefully to some shelter.

2. *Plot.* Our knowledge of the plot is advanced, because we now see that Orlando and Adam have reached the Forest of Arden, in their flight from the wicked Oliver. Orlando's determination to find food for Adam prepares us for his

intrusion into the meal which Duke Senior and his companions are about to enjoy, in the next scene.

If you examine each scene in a similar way, asking yourself how the scene adds to your knowledge of plot and character, you will find that every scene has a purpose, and your understanding of, and respect for, Shakespeare's dramatic craftsmanship will increase.

PLOT

By 'plot', in connection with a book or play, we mean the chain of incidents which is gradually unfolded in the course of the story. Most of you have read *Treasure Island*: the plot of that book could be summarised as:

'The discovery of a map showing the location of Captain Flint's pirate treasure, by a boy named Jim Hawkins, and Jim's adventures during the voyage of the ship *Hispaniola* to recover the treasure.' All the details which come so quickly to your mind, such as Jim's adventure in the apple-barrel, or the attack on the stockade, are parts of the plot; and these incidents are like the links in the chain.

It may happen that, subsidiary to the main story of the book or play, other stories of less importance are mingled. In *Henry V*, for example, subordinate to the main plot dealing with Henry's exploits against the French, we find the comic sub-plot which traces the adventures of Pistol and his rascally comrades. In *As You Like It*, you might consider the courtship of Orlando and Rosalind to be the main plot: then you would notice a number of sub-plots, such as (*a*) Oliver's evil intentions towards his brother, (*b*) Duke Frederick's persecution of Duke Senior, and (*c*) the courtships of Phebe and Silvius, Touchstone and Audrey, and Celia and Oliver. Perhaps you could compare the main plot to a big river, and the sub-plots to tributaries, as the sub-plots are absorbed eventually in the main plot.

Sub-plots complicate the structure of a play, and may

sometimes weaken it because of this; unlikely coincidences or a *deus ex machina*[1] may be necessary to resolve the tangles.

Structure of plot: tragedy. In a tragedy such as *Julius Caesar*, which is uncomplicated by a sub-plot, it is possible to trace the development of the main plot, as it passes through certain accepted stages, which are often given the following titles:

1. Exposition, or Introduction.
2. Complication.
3. Climax, or Turning-point.
4. Resolution.
5. Conclusion, or Catastrophe.

1. *Exposition* is the unfolding of the action of the play, and the introduction of the characters. In *Julius Caesar*, we could say that this takes place in the first Act, when we are made aware of the public admiration for Caesar, and the private hatred and envy of him by Cassius, Casca and their friends. Brutus is afraid that Caesar will be corrupted by the enjoyment of too great power.

2. *Complication* is the gradual increase of the forces which will bring about the climax, and in *Julius Caesar* we might consider it to be the consent of Brutus to join the conspirators, the formation of their plan to murder Caesar, and Caesar's decision to go to the Capitol against the advice of his wife. How long the complication lasts must depend on where we consider the crisis to occur, and here there may be a clash of opinion. Some people may say, in fact, that Caesar's neglect to take his wife's advice is the turning point; others, that his murder marks the climax; while a third group could argue, with reason, that Brutus' decision to allow Antony to speak Caesar's funeral oration, or the oration itself, is the crisis of the play. None of these opinions is necessarily wrong; a play can be analysed into different schemes of plot by different people.

---

[1] The introduction of an unlikely event, in order to escape from some difficulty in the plot.

3. *Climax* is the turning-point of the play, which has a crucial effect on the fortunes of those taking part. Possible climaxes have been mentioned in the previous paragraph.

4. *Resolution* is the gradual working out of the consequences caused by the actions which led up to the Climax. Here, we would notice the flight of the conspirators, the occupation of Rome by the Triumvirate, the quarrel and difficulties of Cassius and Brutus, and the events leading up to the battle of Philippi.

5. *Conclusion* marks the Catastrophe, or downfall of the tragic hero, and in *Julius Caesar*, we might consider this to be either the defeat of the conspirators at Philippi, or the death of Brutus.

It will be noticed in this scheme that the division we have made into phases of action does not necessarily agree with the author's division of the play into Acts; and it is again emphasised that no universally acceptable scheme of the development of a plot can be laid down, since such matters depend, finally, upon individual opinion.

POETRY AND PROSE IN THE PLAYS

BLANK VERSE

On looking at the pages of any of Shakespeare's plays, it is immediately obvious that prose, as we know it in books, is used very little. We notice that Shakespeare's lines, instead of extending fully across the page from margin to margin, vary in length, and we see also that each line begins with a capital letter, exactly like the poetry we have read. This is not surprising, since Shakespeare's plays are written mainly in a form of poetry known as Blank Verse. Before we begin to study this, here is a list of terms that will be used, with explanations:

ACCENT, STRESS. Emphasis on certain syllables, made by voicing them more strongly.

COUPLET. Two lines of verse that rhyme with one another.

FOOT. The division of a line of poetry, consisting of a group of accented and unaccented syllables.

METRE. The regular plan by which a certain number of feet succeed each other in every line of a poem.

RHYME. A similarity in sound between certain words: e.g. thick—stick, when—pen.

RHYTHM. The regular recurrence of accented syllables, which produces a kind of tune, like light and heavy drum beats.

SCAN. To count the feet in verse.

SYLLABLE. Several letters taken together to form one sound: a vowel and one or more consonants; e.g. 'several' consists of three syllables, *sev–er–al*.

The ordinary, or regular, line of blank verse consists of FIVE FEET of TWO SYLLABLES each, the second syllable of each foot being stressed, and the first unstressed. In all, therefore, the line contains TEN syllables.

Here is a line divided into syllables:

He| was| but| as| the| cuc|koo| is| in| June|

(ten syllables).

Here is the same line divided into feet:

He was| but as| the cuc|koo is| in June|

(five feet, each of two syllables).

Now the same line is divided into feet, with the stressed (or accented) syllables marked:

He wás| but ás| the cúc|koo ís| in Júne|.

This verse is called 'blank' because it is unrhymed:

He was but as the cuckoo is in June,
Heard, not regarded; seen, but with such eyes
As, sick and blunted with community,
Afford no extraordinary gaze,
Such as is bent on sun-like majesty
When it shines seldom in admiring eyes.[1]

Practise counting the syllables in lines, and dividing the lines into feet, with the stresses marked.

[1] *Henry IV, Part I*, III, ii, 75–80.

22

Before you have scanned many lines, you will discover that some of them do not fit into the verse scheme given above. Perhaps you will find that the strong stress appears to fall on the first instead of on the second syllable in a foot; or perhaps the line contains more than ten syllables. These are two of the most common irregularities, and are not accidental, but are intended to give variety, and prevent strict regularity of line and rhythm boring the audience and making it weary. Here is an example of the first irregularity, which is called 'inverted stress':

Bátter| his skúll,| or páunch| hím with| a stáke|.[1]

You can see that in the first and fourth feet the stress has moved from the second to the first syllable. When the second irregularity occurs, the extra syllable at the end of the line is usually an unstressed one, and this is known as a double, or feminine, ending:

The| clouds| me|thought| would| op|en| and| show| ri|ches|[2]
(eleven syllables).

The percentage of double endings in a play helps scholars to fix the date of the play, since in Shakespeare's later work the number of these endings is greater than in his early plays. You may even find twelve syllables in a line; this irregularity is also the sign of a later play.

Not only does the feminine ending give variety by breaking the regularity of the ten-syllable line, but also, where there is no pause after it, carries on the sense and rhythm of the speech to the next line. When one line runs on, in sense and movement, into the next line, it is called a 'run-on' line.

> We are such stuff
> As dreams are made on, and our little life
> Is rounded with a sleep.[3]

[1] *The Tempest*, III, ii, 101.   [2] *The Tempest*, III, ii, 153.
[3] *The Tempest*, IV, i, 148–50.

If, however, sense and rhythm are not carried on from one line to the next, the lines are said to be 'end-stopt'. Constant variation between run-on and end-stopt lines is another thing which gives continual life and interest to blank verse.

There are many other ways by which Shakespeare gives variety to his blank verse, about which you can read for yourselves if the subject interests you (see Reading List). The study of Metre is a technical matter, and all that has been attempted here is to satisfy some of the immediate curiosity of enquiring minds. One very useful thing to remember is that when you are quoting several lines of blank verse, and are in doubt where each line ends, you have a fairly safe guide in your knowledge of metre: count off five feet, and that will be the end of your first line, and proceed in this way to the end of your quotation. Assuming that you started at the beginning of a line, and that the lines are regular, you will not be likely to make a serious error.

USE OF RHYME

Although Shakespeare soon discovered that he could express himself most freely and naturally in blank verse, in the plays that he wrote first, such as *Love's Labour's Lost*, he used a high proportion of rhymed lines. As his skill in writing blank verse increased, perhaps he felt that rhyme was artificial, or lacking in variety, or tiring to the ear: at any rate, he gradually stopped using it, except in songs or for special purposes, and the later plays have little rhyme in them. It is a safe test of the date of a play to see whether there is much rhyme in it, or not; if there is, the play is early; if there is not, the play was written later in Shakespeare's life.

In all the plays, rhyme is used, generally speaking, as follows:

(a) *At the end of a scene.* A rhymed couplet served the important purpose of marking the end of a scene. This was necessary at a time when plays were performed without drop-curtains or changes of scenery, and evidently became a convention accepted by the audience.

> A fortnight hold we this solemnity
> In nightly revels, and new jollity,[1]

says Duke Theseus, at the end of scene i of Act v, *A Midsummer Night's Dream*.

(b) *At the conclusion of a train of thought, or in farewell.* The couplet often sums up the situation and expresses it in a pointed way, which would be more noticeable by the audience. The Duchess of York ends her cursing of King Richard III by summarising her feelings thus:

> Bloody thou art, bloody will be thy end;
> Shame serves thy life and doth thy death attend.[2]

Kent, saying farewell after his banishment by King Lear, uses the following couplet:

> Thus Kent, O princes! bids you all adieu;
> He'll shape his old course in a country new.[3]

(c) *To express a proverbial saying.* A stronger effect is gained, and the memory assisted, by the use of a couplet to express proverbs. Rhyme is frequently the natural form for traditional sayings. When Phebe falls in love with Rosalind, who is disguised as a young man, she quotes from Marlowe

> Dead shepherd, now I find thy saw of might:
> 'Whoever lov'd that lov'd not at first sight?'[4]

(d) *To express intention or resolution.* John of Gaunt determines to help Richard to pacify Mowbray and Bolingbroke:

> To be a make-peace shall become my age:
> Throw down, my son, the Duke of Norfolk's gage.[5]

[1] Ll. 378–9. [2] *Richard III*, IV, iv, 195–6.
[3] *King Lear*, I, i, 189–90. [4] *As You Like It*, III, v, 81–2.
[5] *Richard II*, I, i, 160–1.

Although it is unsafe to generalise, Shakespeare normally uses prose when he wishes to lower the dramatic pitch: verse was evidently considered more high sounding and suitable for the expression of noble thoughts. From instances in the plays, it appears that Shakespeare employed prose mainly for the following special purposes:

1. For letters, and other documents.
2. In comic scenes.
3. For the conversation of people of humble position.
4. In scenes depicting madness.

Let us consider each separately.

1. *Letters.* There are many examples of prose being used in documents. When Lady Macbeth receives a letter from Macbeth, after the battle, it is written in prose:

> They met me in the day of success; and I have learned by the perfectest report, they have more in them than mortal knowledge

it begins, describing the first meeting with the witches. And Artemidorus wrote his warning to Caesar in prose:

> Caesar, beware of Brutus; take heed of Cassius; come not near Casca; have an eye to Cinna; trust not Trebonius; mark well Metellus Cimber; Decius Brutus loves thee not; thou hast wronged Caius Ligarius.[2]

2. *Comic scenes.* Prose is normally spoken throughout comic scenes, and Touchstone, the Clown in *As You Like It*, uses it to the exclusion of blank verse. In *Macbeth*, the Porter speaks in prose, and so do Lady Macduff and her son in the humorous dialogue between them. The wooing of Henry V is carried on in prose, and it is interesting to notice the change from verse to prose: Henry first addresses Katharine in formal blank verse:

> Fair Katharine, and most fair!
> Will you vouchsafe to teach a soldier terms,

---

[1] *Macbeth*, I, v, 1–3.
[2] *Julius Caesar*, II, iii, 1–5.

> Such as will enter at a lady's ear,
> And plead his love-suit to her gentle heart?[1]

But, on receiving her reply, in broken English, and in prose,

> Your majesty sall mock at me; I cannot speak your England,

he abandons blank verse for the informality of prose, and does not return to it until Westmoreland introduces the important matter of the terms of the treaty with France.

3. *Conversation of humble characters.* As a general rule, people of low birth and position speak naturally in prose while those of superior rank speak in blank verse. Thus, we find the soldiers in *Henry V*, the Roman citizens in *Julius Caesar*, and the frequenters of the Boar's Head Tavern in *Henry IV, Parts I and II*, conversing in prose. Exceptions occur:

(*a*) When a humble character brings important news, or has something to say which temporarily increases his importance, or is dignified by speaking to someone of high rank: thus, messengers normally speak in blank verse because of the news they bear; and old Adam's usual prose is raised to the level of blank verse by the dignity he shows in his loyalty to Orlando.

(*b*) When a person of low birth pretends to be more important than he really is (often for humorous purposes). In this way, Pistol shows his pretensions to valour and rank by speaking in bombastic verse.

(*c*) When a person of high rank condescends to speak to someone of low rank, and consequently uses prose; for example, Henry V, in disguise, talking to his soldiers; Rosalind conversing with Touchstone; or Edgar, in *King Lear*, pretending to be a country fellow.

4. *Scenes depicting madness.* Shakespeare frequently uses prose to indicate an abnormal mental state: the sleep-walking scene in *Macbeth* (Act v, sc. i), where Lady Macbeth shows that

[1] *Henry V*, v, ii, 98–103.

her reason has been disturbed by her guilty conscience, is an example of this. Hamlet, pretending to be mad, and poor Ophelia, mad indeed, provide other instances.

FIGURES OF SPEECH

Only the Figures of Speech and Dramatic Figures which are most frequently met are explained here, in the hope that an understanding of them may add to the appreciation and interest of the student who comes across them in the course of his reading.

ALLITERATION

This name is given to the recurrence of the same sound at the beginning of two or more words in close succession. Often this is brought about by the recurrence of the same letter, but not necessarily so.

Alliteration is used mainly to give additional force to words; in *Richard III*, when Queen Elizabeth is advising the Marquess of Dorset to flee, she says

> O, Dorset! speak not to me, get thee gone;
> Death and destruction dog thee at the heels.[1]

There, the alliterative sound is 'D'; and it would be hard to resist so forcible an appeal.

HYPERBOLE

When Macbeth, after he has murdered King Duncan, declares that all the water in the sea will never wash his hands clean again, he is obviously exaggerating, and to this type of exaggeration we give the name hyperbole.

> Will all great Neptune's ocean wash this blood
> Clean from my hand? No, this my hand will rather
> The multitudinous seas incarnadine,
> Making the green one red.[2]

[1] *Richard III*, IV, i, 38–9.   [2] *Macbeth*, II, ii, 61–4.

28

This consists in a transference of meaning, the setting down of one thing for another which it only resembles, to obtain a more graphic picture. Instead of calling England an island surrounded by water, John of Gaunt speaks of it as

This precious stone set in the silver sea,[1]

thus giving us a much more elaborate and brilliant picture. We use metaphors frequently, without being aware of it; when we say that someone spoke sharply to us, we are using a simple metaphorical figure, since we have transferred the word 'sharp' from its proper use as descriptive of cutting implements, to show that the words used to us were equally 'cutting'. Unfortunately, many of the metaphors current in ordinary conversation are 'hackneyed'—that is to say, they have been used so often that they have lost much of their original freshness and force. Simile (see the note on this figure) is implicit in a metaphor; in the example from *Richard II* given above, Gaunt means that England is *like* a precious stone set in the silver sea.

MIXED METAPHOR

You should be careful to avoid mixing your metaphors accidentally, as by so doing you will avoid a mistake which is often humorous in its effect, and may sometimes be used to gain that effect deliberately. Shakespeare occasionally slips, unintentionally, though some of his mixed metaphors seem to gain strength and effect from the fact that they are mixed:

Or to take arms against a sea of troubles.[2]

No doubt the error is obvious; to have completed consistently the metaphor of taking arms (or fighting), the troubles should have been thought of as an army.

[1] *Richard II*, II, i, 46. [2] *Hamlet*, III, i, 58.

This is the formation of a word to resemble the sound of the thing of which it is the name; 'cuckoo', for example, is the name of a bird whose cry echoes the sound of its name; and if you were told that the word 'agwagwa' was the name of a bird, ignorance of the Hausa language would hardly prevent you from guessing that it meant 'Duck', so truly does the name follow the sound.

In Shakespeare's plays, the application of Onomatopoeia is not to the *formation* of words, but to the *use* of words which, in their sound, resemble the thing they describe. Anne, who is to be crowned Richard's queen against her will, wishes that the crown was red-hot and would kill her; notice how the sound of her words, and the repetition of the 's' sound in particular, convey to your mind the hiss of red-hot, burning metal:

> O! would to God that the inclusive verge
> Of golden metal that must round my brow
> Were red-hot steel to sear me to the brain.[1]

In addition, you will notice in some lines that the use of long heavy syllables makes the line drag slowly, and thus conveys the idea of weariness or sorrow, while the use of short words with the quickly following syllables gives the impression of happiness or haste.

PATHETIC FALLACY

The Greek word 'pathos' means 'feeling', and pathetic fallacy is the erroneous feeling or belief that happenings in the world of Nature have any intentional connection with human lives. In many parts of the world it is believed that a falling star indicates the death of some great man: this is an example of the pathetic fallacy, since there is no scientific proof that natural phenomena can influence human lives, except

[1] *Richard III*, IV, i, 58–60.

accidentally. Calphurnia voices the belief in advising Caesar not to go to the Capitol:

> When beggars die there are no comets seen;
> The heavens themselves blaze forth the death of princes.[1]

It is interesting to note in this connection that Harry Percy (Hotspur), in *Henry IV, Part I*, makes fun of Glendower, who believes that his own birth was marked by earthquakes and signs in the sky:

Glendower.   ...and at my birth
The frame and huge foundations of the earth
Shak'd like a coward.
Hotspur. Why, so it would have done at the same season, if
your mother's cat had but kittened, though yourself had
never been born.[2]

PERSONIFICATION

In order to make an abstract thing appear more real to us, it is sometimes spoken of in literature as though it was a living person; thus, Shakespeare, in *Macbeth*, speaks of murder as if it was a human being, old and walking with silent steps to carry out its purpose:

> ...and wither'd murder,
> Alarum'd by his sentinel, the wolf,
> Whose howl's his watch, thus with his stealthy pace,
> With Tarquin's ravishing strides, toward his design
> Moves like a ghost.[3]

PROLEPSIS

In this figure an action which is to be performed in the future is spoken of as though it has already taken place: before he goes to murder King Duncan, Macbeth says:

> I go, and it is done.[4]

In fact, the murder has not yet been carried out, but Macbeth speaks as if he has already accomplished it.

[1] *Julius Caesar*, II, ii, 30–31.   [2] *Henry IV, Part I*, III, i, 15–20.
[3] *Macbeth*, II, i, 52–6.   [4] *Macbeth*, II, i, 62.

PUN

A pun is a joke made by using two words which are similar in sound but different in meaning to produce a humorous effect. The word 'guilt', for instance, has the same sound as the word 'gilt' (past participle of the verb to gild), but their meaning is quite different. Thus, when Lady Macbeth says:

> ... If he do bleed,
> I'll gild the faces of the grooms withal;
> For it must seem their guilt.[1]

she is making use of the word 'guilt' to convey the two ideas:

(*a*) that the grooms are guilty, and

(*b*) that their faces are gilt.

The Elizabethan audience was very fond of such playing on words, and Shakespeare makes many puns in his plays. To the modern taste, continual indulgence in punning becomes rather tedious, though the best puns can show a very subtle wit.

SIMILE

This is one of the most common, and yet the most effective, of literary figures, but it should be remembered that a simile should be both fresh and graphic if it is to help your description. It consists of a comparison which, it is hoped, will make the object described more clear and bright to the reader or listener. A simile is nearly always introduced by the words 'as' or, 'like', so it is easy to recognise:

> Was this the face
> That like the sun did make beholders wink?[2]

says King Richard II, contrasting his past glory with his present misery.

---

[1] *Macbeth*, II, ii, 56–68.
[2] *Richard II*, IV, i, 283–4.

ANACHRONISM

This means a mistake in regard to time, by which something is assigned to an earlier or to a later age than the one to which it really belongs: if you were writing an account of the Battle of Hastings, and you said that King Harold was killed by the bullet from a gun, this would be an anachronism, since gunpowder was unknown in England in the eleventh century. Shakespeare occasionally makes a mistake of this kind: in *Julius Caesar*, Cassius says

> The clock hath stricken [struck] three,[1]

whereas there were no striking clocks in the Rome of that time.

THE TRAGIC HERO

It is usually assumed that the unfortunate, and possibly fatal, accidents which concern almost everyone at some period or other are of limited interest to observers. Perhaps they are too commonplace; perhaps the fact that they happen to ordinary people like ourselves makes them seem less striking. The effect is much more terrible if the disaster occurs to someone, who, by reason of his high rank, wealth or fame, seemed armoured against Fate. By contrast, his fall is more awe-inspiring, more tragic.

The first requisite, then, of the tragic hero, is that he should be a person of such note that the calamity which overcomes him will give us a feeling of awe, almost of terror. He may be a king, or a noble, a famous soldier, a person of position and power. He is no common, ordinary man. He appears secure, unassailable.

Among the virtues possessed by the hero, there is a weakness or fault (the Tragic Flaw, or Tragic Fault). It is not a weakness or vice which, in itself, need be very serious. It is

[1] *Julius Caesar*, II, i, 192.

the sort of weakness which we all possess, such as pride, ambition, indecisiveness, or jealousy, and which we take through life with us, without it ever doing us too much harm. Acted on by the circumstances which surround the hero, however, it proves fatal to him; and the more homely and universal and harmless the failing, the more tragic and wasteful does the disaster appear. To some extent, also, our sympathy with the tragic hero, and consequently our estimate of the success of the play, is governed by our acceptance and understanding of his tragic flaw. By the scholarly dreamer, Hamlet's character may be easily understood, and his downfall pitied; to the man of action, Hamlet may seem weak and vacillating, Macbeth a truly tragic figure. The wider our understanding, the more universal our sympathy will be, the more credible the tragic fault.

Circumstances outside the control of the hero play an important part in aggravating the effect of his weakness and bringing about his ruin. In *Macbeth*, for example, the hero's ambition and superstition are acted upon by his unscrupulous wife and the antagonistic witches: then, by chance, an opportunity occurs for Macbeth to put into action his evil thoughts, and he sets in train the events which lead to his destruction. In Tragedy, it has been said, we see the individual overwhelmed by his environment.

> So, oft it chances in particular men,
> That for some *vicious mole of nature in them*,[1]
> As, in their birth,—wherein they are not guilty,
> Since nature cannot choose *his*[2] origin,—
> By the o'ergrowth of some *complexion*,[3]
> Oft breaking down the *pales*[4] and forts of reason,
> Or by some habit that *too much o'er leavens*[5]
> The form of *plausive*[6] manners; that these men,

[1] Some natural blemish. [2] Its.
[3] Natural tendency of character.
[4] Boundaries.
[5] Changes too strongly. [6] Attractive.

34

Carrying, I say, the stamp of one defect,
Being nature's *livery*[1], or fortune's star,
Their virtues else, be they as pure as grace,
As infinite as man may undergo,
Shall in *the general censure*[2] *take corruption*[3]
From that particular fault.[4]

Though the construction of this passage is not very easy, it expresses strongly and clearly the idea that one defect, which a person may have through no fault of his own, can gradually spoil all his other splendid virtues, as one bad fruit can infect all the good fruit in a heap with its rottenness.

DRAMATIC IRONY

Simple Irony, unlike Dramatic Irony, is purely verbal, and in its usual form consists of saying the opposite of what you mean, to produce a sarcastic or humorous effect: for example, Antony, describing the conspirators, against whom he hopes to anger the crowd of citizens, and meaning to imply that the conspirators are traitors, says

So are they all, all honourable men.[5]

Dramatic Irony, on the other hand, is a situation rather than a merely verbal figure. Sometimes known also as Tragic Irony, it consists of a situation in a play (or book) in which a character shows by his remarks that he is ignorant of some misfortune hanging over him. The audience, and sometimes other characters in the play, know, or have guessed, certain facts which make the speaker's ignorance clear to them, and therefore the speaker's words have a second meaning or significance which is hidden from him, but is seen by the others.

---

[1] Uniform.
[2] Final estimate.
[3] Be spoiled by.
[4] *Hamlet*, I, iv, 23–36.
[5] *Julius Caesar*, III, ii, 89.

3-2

Caesar, on his way to the Capitol, asks Trebonius to stay close to him for a talk:

Be near me, that I may remember you.[1]

Only Caesar is ignorant of the fact that Trebonius is one of the conspirators who intend to kill him at the Capitol, and who will therefore be near to him, though for a very different purpose than that intended by Caesar.

Situations of this kind can greatly increase the dramatic impact of a play, and can be used to heighten either tragedy or comedy. It adds to the excitement of the audience to feel the suspense of seeing one of the characters walking, as it were, unsuspectingly into an ambush without being able to warn him.

Much amusement is derived from the scene in *Henry IV, Part I*, where Falstaff tells the Prince and Poins how he has been robbed and beaten by fourteen men, when really, as the audience knows, the Prince and Poins, in disguise, had robbed him themselves.

The Dramatic Irony in a situation is not always immediately apparent; that is to say, sometimes we do not perceive the Irony until we look back upon a speaker's words with the added knowledge that future events give us. After the murder of Duncan, Lady Macbeth says:

A little water clears us of this deed.[2]

No Dramatic Irony is then perceptible; but later in the play, when she is sleep-walking, and her brain is turning, she imagines that her hands are still stained with blood:

What! will these hands ne'er be clean?[3]

The water was not sufficient to wash the deed from her conscience.

[1] *Julius Caesar*, II, ii, 123. [2] *Macbeth*, II, ii, 68.
[3] *Macbeth*, V, i, 47–8.

COMIC RELIEF

To witness the performance of a tragedy on the stage can cause a considerable emotional strain; in fact, Aristotle went so far as to say that the final effect on our feelings is comparable to the effect produced on our bodies by taking a purge. If you have seen a tragedy acted well, you will know that it is true to say that you leave the theatre feeling cleansed; your mind has been humbled, but at the same time your thoughts are ennobled, and you feel better and wiser.

Evidently, then, the author of a tragedy is working on our emotions and feelings. His aim is to produce a tragic effect. Yet it is a peculiar fact that tragedy is not produced by heaping sorrow on sorrow: there is a limit to the unhappiness an audience can bear, and if this limit is exceeded the audience will find its own relief, either by going away, or by laughing at the wrong moment. Either of these actions would spell the failure of the play. To avoid this, Shakespeare introduces humorous scenes into his tragedies, so that the audience can obtain relief, by laughter, from the surrounding gloom of the tragedy, without the impact of the tragedy being accidentally reduced.

The first purpose, then, of this dramatic device, is to give the audience relief in laughter. The second purpose is not so obvious. The tragedy has reached a critical and perhaps terrifying point, when suddenly we are invited to laugh. Now, although we are glad of the relief, at the back of our minds we are wondering what is going to happen in the tragedy; and as the comic relief scene progresses, our impatience and anxiety increase, so that the second function of the scene is finally to increase the tragic effect.

A diagram, based on *Macbeth*, might make this clearer (see p. 38).

The functions of Comic Relief can be summarised, therefore, thus: (*a*) to reduce the strain on the audience by providing a safety valve to allow the escape of emotion and excitement, and (*b*) gradually to increase the tension to an even higher level, by leading us to wonder what is happening or what is going to happen in the main plot.

Its effect is like switching on the light in a dark room: the light relieves the gloom momentarily, but when the light is extinguished the darkness seems blacker.

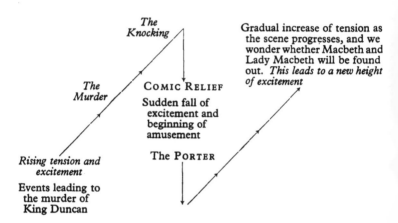

The
Knocking

Gradual increase of tension as the scene progresses, and we wonder whether Macbeth and Lady Macbeth will be found out. *This leads to a new height of excitement*

The
Murder

COMIC RELIEF

Sudden fall of excitement and beginning of amusement

The PORTER

Rising tension and excitement

Events leading to the murder of King Duncan

THE PART OF THE FOOL

In several of the plays, tragedies as well as comedies, we find professional Fools, or Clowns, appearing. Their accomplishments and characteristics in Shakespeare seem similar to those of the professional Fools who lived at Court, or in the households of great men, during the Elizabethan Age.

(*a*) They are witty and amusing. Hamlet describes Yorick, the jester, as 'a fellow of infinite jest, of most excellent fancy', and, now that Yorick is dead, Hamlet asks 'Where be your jibes now? your gambols? your songs? your flashes of merriment, that were wont to set the table on a roar?'[1]

[1] *Hamlet*, v, i, 202–3, and 207–10.

(b) They are shrewd observers and commentators on the behaviour of others, and are given the privilege of censuring foolishness, even if it is the foolishness of their own masters. If they go too far, however, they run the risk of punishment. Touchstone, conversing with Celia, insinuates that her father, Duke Frederick, has a dishonourable friend, and Celia rebukes him—

My father's love is enough to honour him. Enough! speak no more of him; you'll be whipped for taxation one of these days,

whereupon Touchstone aptly replies:

The more pity, that fools may not speak wisely what wise men do foolishly.[1]

Jaques, on a later occasion, speaks of 'he that a fool doth very wisely hit',[2] so it is evident much of their wit consisted of mockery of individual follies and idiosyncrasies.

(c) They are able to entertain with songs and verse. Feste, the Clown in *Twelfth Night*, is called upon to sing, and is praised for his 'mellifluous voice'.[3] Touchstone is quick to parody the verses which Orlando has written to Rosalind.

(d) They are pictured, by Shakespeare, as being loyal and affectionate. Celia says, of Touchstone,

He'll go along o'er the wide world with me,[4]

and the Fool, in *King Lear*, is the King's faithful and solitary companion throughout the storm,

who labours to out-jest
His heart-struck injuries.[5]

Viola, in *Twelfth Night*, speaking of Feste the Clown, summarises the duties and accomplishments of the Fool:

This fellow's wise enough to play the fool,
And to do that well craves a kind of wit:

[1] *As You Like It*, I, ii, 90–4.　　[2] *As You Like It*, II, vii, 53.
[3] *Twelfth Night*, II, iii, 56.　　[4] *As You Like It*, I, iii, 135.
[5] *King Lear*, III, i, 16–17.

He must observe their mood on whom he jests,
The quality of persons, and the time,
Not, like the haggard, check at every feather
That comes before his eye. This is a practice
As full of labour as a wise man's art.[1]

THE SONGS

Shakespeare introduces songs into his Comedies and Tragedies,
and it seems likely that, if one of the boy actors in the company
had a particularly pleasing voice, Shakespeare would deliberately
include songs for him in the play on which he was working at
that time. In both Tragedies and Comedies, however, the
striking thing is the aptness of the songs: they are appropriate
in their words and mood to the action of the scene in which
they occur, and this makes their introduction seem natural
and unforced.

In the Comedies, the main object of the songs is to entertain
the audience; and the songs are, in fact, of such quality that
they give great pleasure. Autolycus, the wandering pedlar,
sings as he walks along:

> Jog on, jog on, the footpath way,
> And merrily hent the stile-a:
> A merry heart goes all the day,
> Your sad tires in a mile-a,[2]

and his words are appropriate to his situation: Amiens sings
of life under the greenwood tree, when he is in exile with
Duke Senior in the Forest of Arden; while Feste sings that
'journeys end in lovers meeting',[3] forecasting the conclusion
of *Twelfth Night*.

The songs in the Tragedies heighten the tragic effect. Thus,

[1] *Twelfth Night*, III, i, 68–74.
[2] *Winter's Tale*, IV, ii, 133–6.
[3] *Twelfth Night*, II, iii, 46.

Ophelia, in her madness, touches our emotions with her pitiful songs; as Laertes says:

> Hadst thou thy wits, and didst persuade revenge,
> It could not move thus.

And later he comments:

> Thought and affliction, passion, hell itself,
> She turns to favour and to prettiness.[1]

The pathos of the scene in which Desdemona is preparing for bed, on the night that Othello murders her, is heightened by the song she sings; and our apprehension and foreboding are increased by the tragic shadow which she can sense herself:

> My mother had a maid call'd Barbara,
> She was in love, and he she lov'd prov'd mad
> And did forsake her; she had a song of 'willow';
> An old thing 'twas, but it express'd her fortune,
> And she died singing it; that song tonight
> Will not go from my mind. . . .[2]

[1] *Hamlet*, IV, v, 167–8, and 187–8.
[2] *Othello*, IV, iii, 26–31.

The Theatre

THE MODERN THEATRE

In most parts of the world, perhaps especially in Africa, there is a strong acting tradition, and great eagerness to give dramatic performances. But these traditions and performances are usually very different from the techniques evolved through the years, and now used as standard practice, in the modern European theatre. Consequently, those of you who are oversea students cannot be expected to have any mental picture of a conventional stage, or knowledge of its possibilities and limitations. It is important, in studying Shakespeare's plays, never to lose sight of the fact that the plays were written for acting and not for reading. Some idea of the stage and theatre in the time of Shakespeare is necessary, and it is to help students to understand more easily Elizabethan stage-craft, when reference is made to it, that these brief notes on the modern theatre and the Elizabethan theatre have been included, with pictures and a short list of theatrical terms.

From Fig. 1 you notice that the audience and the actors are quite separate; in fact, as you will see from Figs. 2 and 3, the stage is built up on a platform several feet high. The chief reason for this elevation is so that people at the rear of the audience can see as well as those in front.

The *wings* are concealed from the audience by walls or curtains, and in them are to be found articles of scenery, lighting equipment, dressing rooms for the actors and the prompter (see list of theatrical terms).

Above the *proscenium* there is an arch, and here hang the

front curtains, which completely hide the stage from the view of the audience, except when they are drawn back for the play to begin.

The *auditorium* is kept in darkness during the performance, so that the stage lighting is more brilliant by contrast. The main methods of lighting the stage are by *footlights*, *floats* and *spotlights*.

(*a*) Footlights. These are lights at the edge of the stage, and level with the floor of the stage, extending the full width, and concealed from the audience by a kind of ledge.

(*b*) Floats. These lights are placed behind the proscenium arch, and shine downwards on the actors.

(*c*) Spotlights. By means of these lights, the face of a particular actor, or part of the stage, can be illuminated separately.

There are controls to vary the brilliance of all lights, so that it is easy to give the impression, say, of sunset or sunrise.

The stage itself is set out to represent the scene which is being acted. By means of canvas screens (*flats*), which can be painted in a very realistic way (Fig. 3) and which are light to move about and easy to store, landscapes, houses, rooms and so on, can be simulated. Painted sheets hanging from above can give an illusion of clouds. Real furniture is used. Apparatus can be made for almost every kind of exit and entrance, and even the illusion of flying can be provided. Some theatres have revolving stages, on which several scenes can be set up; as soon as one scene is finished, the stage is rotated, and at once the next scene appears. Even this short description has perhaps enabled you to realise that there is very little impossible to the modern stage engineer, and some of the effects are almost magical.

List of useful stage terms

ACTORS. Those who act in a play.

AUDIENCE. Those who listen to, and watch, a play.

AUDITORIUM. The part of the theatre occupied by the audience, and separate from the stage.

BOX-OFFICE. The place from which tickets for the play are bought.

CURTAIN. The curtain separating the stage from the audience.

DRESSING-ROOMS. The rooms in which the actors change their clothes and get ready.

FLATS. Flat screens painted to represent scenes; scenery.

FLIES. Curtains hanging above the stage to represent clouds and sky, ceilings, etc.

FLOATS. Lights shining down on to the stage from behind the proscenium arch.

FOOTLIGHTS. Lights on a level with the actor's feet.

MAKE-UP. The artificial colouring of the actors' faces and addition of false hair, beards, etc., to make them resemble the character they are intended to represent.

PRODUCER. The person responsible for the production and interpretation of the play as a whole.

PROMPTER. The person who sits concealed in the wings and quietly whispers the words to any actor who forgets his lines.

PROPERTIES. Articles used in the play, such as Shylock's knife, or the Dauphin's tennis balls.

PROSCENIUM ARCH. The arch which frames the upper part of the stage space.

SPOTLIGHT. A light which can illuminate a particular person or section of the stage.

STAGE. The raised platform on which the actors stand.

STAGE HANDS. Men who help in the work, such as scene-shifting.

STAGE MANAGER. The man responsible for the setting, etc., of the stage.

WARDROBE MISTRESS. The woman who looks after all the clothes used in the play.

WIGS. False hair, on a cloth scalp, which the actor may wear to hide his own hair and resemble someone else.

WINGS. The sides of the stage concealed from the audience.

Remember that actors and actresses have to learn their parts in the play entirely by heart.

Fig. 1.

1, 2 Business offices.
3 Ledge for a spotlight.
4 Prompter (in the wings).
5 Properties (in the wings).

6 Stage hand working the flies.
7 Stacked scenery; flats.
8 Wardrobe.
9 Stage.

10, 11 Dressing rooms.
12, 13, } Stage offices and
14, 15 } workshops.
16 Horizontal beams from which are hung the flies.

Fig. 2. Model of the new theatre at Coventry, the first to be built in England for twenty-five years. Every seat will command a good view of the stage. It is a small, intimate theatre.

THE ELIZABETHAN THEATRE

The Elizabethan theatre (see Fig. 5) was different from the modern theatre in the following important particulars:

(*a*) The apron stage projected into the audience, and it was impossible to separate the stage from the audience, as there was no proscenium curtain to drop.

(*b*) There was no set scenery.

(*c*) The female parts were played by boys: no women took part in the plays.

These points influenced Shakespeare in his writing and construction, and some understanding of them will increase our appreciation of his technique. Let us examine them separately.

(*a*) *The Apron Stage.* As the audience was grouped round the apron stage on three sides, with some of the privileged

46

Fig. 3. Royal Opera House, Covent Garden, London. This picture shows how the proscenium arch divides the actors from the audience. You can see the orchestra between the audience and the stage. Compare the very elaborate scenery with the bare Elizabethan stage.

gallants actually sitting on the stage itself, the actors were in full view all the time that they were on the stage. This gave the playwright the problem of removing any bodies from the stage in a way which could be accepted by the audience without any feeling of unreality. It is interesting to note the methods which Shakespeare adopts when he presents a death upon the stage. When Hamlet dies, his body is carried from the stage in a solemn procession:

> Let four captains
> Bear Hamlet, like a soldier, to the stage...
> ...   .
> Take up the bodies.[1]
> > [*A dead march. Exeunt, bearing off the bodies.*

[1] *Hamlet*, v, ii, 409–10, 415.

Polonius is carried off stage by Hamlet, who has killed him, in the interests of the plot:

> I'll lug the guts into the neighbour room.[1]

Thus, the audience is spared the unnatural spectacle of seeing the apparently dead come to life and walk away.

The end of a scene, which could not be marked by the fall of a proscenium curtain, was shown instead by a rhyming couplet at the end of the final speech in the scene: for example, Henry V, speaking after the surrender of Harfleur, marks the end of the scene in his words:

> Tonight in Harfleur will we be your *guest*;
> To-morrow for the march are we *address*.[2]

This was a convention understood and accepted by the Elizabethan audience.

(b) *Absence of Scenery*. Although 'props' (properties) such as furniture, rocks, thrones and so on were used on the stage, the absence of set scenery meant that the audience had to use its imagination to supply what its eyes could not see. Shakespeare himself provided pictorial descriptions in the dialogue of the plays which set the scene. Thus, Banquo tells us it is a starless night:

> There's husbandry in heaven;
> Their candles are all out,[3]

and Horatio pictures the dawn which there were no lighting effects to simulate:

> But look, the morn in russet mantle clad,
> Walks o'er the dew of yon high eastern hill,[4]

and our imagination at once fills in the detail. So evocative are Shakespeare's words, that scenery was unnecessary.

(c) *Boy Actors in Female Parts*. Although no women took part in the plays, Shakespeare did not limit or restrict his

[1] *Hamlet*, III, iv, 212.   [2] *Henry V*, III, iii, 57–8.
[3] *Macbeth*, II, i, 4–5.   [4] *Hamlet*, I, i, 166–7.

48

female characterisation. To see a competent production of a Shakespearean play at a boys' school is to realise that boys can play the female characters most convincingly. And, as we have seen, if there was a boy in the company of actors with a fine singing voice, Shakespeare might include songs in his part for the boy to sing. In plays such as *As You Like It*, the amusing situation develops of boy actors playing the parts of girls, who, in turn, are pretending to be boys!

Picture of Elizabethan Theatre

If you look at Fig. 5 you will notice that, on either side of the stage, at the back, there is a door, and it was through these two doors that the actors entered. Between the doors hung curtains, known as 'traverses', which could be pulled aside, probably to reveal a recess. This would be used to represent an inner room in a house or some similar dramatic requirement; no doubt, when *The Tempest* was produced, it served as Prospero's cell.

Above the recess may have been a balcony, which would be used as dramatic necessity indicated, or a temporary structure may have been set up on the stage, to serve the purpose. In *Romeo and Juliet*, for instance, it would serve as the balcony in front of Juliet's bedroom. The roof which you can see higher up, the pent-house, or 'heavens', protected the central portion of the stage from rain, for the theatre was open to the sky. Still higher, above the heavens, was the loft, which formed a third storey, and could be used as a station for the trumpeter who signalled the beginning of a play; while, from the turret, a flag was flown several hours before the play started. This was visible from some distance, and served as an advertisement, though posters were also used to inform the citizens that a play was showing. The theatres, along with the bear-gardens, and other places where large congregations of people collected, were situated on the right bank of the River Thames, to minimise the danger of epidemics of plague, and because

THE SWAN THEATRE, BANKSIDE.

Fig. 4. De Witt's drawing of the Swan theatre, Bankside, the only surviving Elizabethan drawing of an Elizabethan theatre.

Fig. 5. Dr Richard Southern's model of a typical Elizabethan public playhouse. Note the apron-stage projecting boldly into the central yard of the building, and compare it with the stage at Coventry or Covent Garden. Look at the model for the following: entrance doors, traverses, balcony, heavens, loft.

the Puritans of the city objected to such forms of entertainment. Admission prices would range from about 10d. to 10s. in our money, 1d. to 1s. in theirs.

The actors changed in a tiring-house behind the stage. They wore usually the Elizabethan dress appropriate to the rank and position of the character they were representing, and made use of false hair, wigs and beards, to show differences in age and sex.

Sudden entrances, such as that of the Ghost in *Macbeth*, and disappearances, such as the witches' cauldron sinking into the ground in the same play, could be engineered quite simply by means of a trap-door in the stage.

Study and Examinations

PUNCTUATION AND READING

Possibly you will not have a chance to act on the stage the play that you are studying. It is even more important, in that case, that you should make the effort of reading the play aloud, taking parts, in class; or, if you are studying by yourself, try to enlist the help of some of your friends to read the play with you. When the words have to be spoken aloud, shades of meaning and dramatic incidents stand out more clearly than they do in silent reading, and sometimes in a different, unexpected, light. Do not worry if you make mistakes, and stumble occasionally; keep going, and try to put yourself into the skin of the character whose part you are playing. Pupils are made self-conscious by a teacher who is continually halting them to point out small mistakes of diction or expression, and if they become self-conscious, the hope of arousing any excitement in their reading of the play is gone.

Attention to some small points may help to make your reading more enjoyable:

(a) Follow the punctuation carefully, otherwise you will make nonsense of the text. Forget about the rhythm; after a while you will unconsciously begin to feel that.

Here is a short passage, with explanations of how you should observe the punctuation:

> I pray you, in your letters,
> When you shall these unlucky deeds relate,
> Speak of me as I am; nothing extenuate,

> Nor set down aught in malice: then, must you speak—→
> Of one that lov'd not wisely but too well.[1]

, Slight pause, with the voice kept up in pitch.

; A longer pause, with the voice allowed to sink, and a breath taken.

: A long pause, with a good breath, ready for the run-on line.

→ No pause at the end of this line; the line is run-on in sympathy with the sense of the sentence.

(A slight intake of breath is possible at commas: breathing should, as far as you can make it, be imperceptible.)

(*b*) At the end of a word '—ed' is normally pronounced as a separate syllable:

And| let| our| ar|my| be| dis|charg|ed| too|[2]   (ten syllables),

but '—'d' indicates that no extra syllable is required:

And| when| you| are| de|sir|ous| to| be| bless'd| (ten syllables)
I'll blessing beg of you.[3]

(*c*) Apostrophes indicate that a letter is omitted, and consequently a syllable, as the missing letter is not pronounced:

  I| think| up|on't|, I| think,| I| smell't|; O| vil|lan|y| !⁴
                                      (twelve syllables)

and in a line like this, with two extra syllables, the last two syllables are not accented, but allowed to fade.

LEARNING BY HEART

The custom of learning by heart does not seem so widely practised as it was, but time spent in learning the great speeches in the play you are studying will not be wasted. At worst, you will have a sense of achievement: at best, you will have some lastingly enjoyable furniture for your mind.

---

[1] *Othello*, V, ii, 339–43.
[2] *Henry IV, Part II*, IV, ii, 92.
[3] *Hamlet*, III, iv, 171–2.
[4] *Othello*, V, ii, 189.

Taking *As You Like It* as an example, learning by heart is suggested on the following scale:

> All the Songs.
> Act II, sc. i, ll. 1–18.
>   sc. iii, ll. 56–68.
>   sc. vii, ll. 12–34, and 139–66.
> Act IV, sc. i, ll. 11–21, and
> Act V, sc. iv, ll. 94–109.

It will be noticed that these passages represent, not only some of the great speeches, but some interesting aspects of the play, such as the 'degrees of a lie', and may therefore be useful for examination purposes.

PARAPHRASING

This consists of rewriting a passage, chosen from one of the plays, in modern English. Paraphrases are not important in the School Certificate Examination, so there is no necessity to prepare especially for such questions. Practice in paraphrasing provides, however, a valuable exercise in clear expression, and a reliable test of whether you really understand the passage chosen. It is often easy to think that you understand a speech, but it may prove extremely difficult to put down, in your own words, what you thought previously was so clear. It is recommended, therefore, that students should paraphrase passages from the plays they are studying, beginning with simple passages, and progressing to those of greater difficulty.

Here are a few hints:

(*a*) Read over the passage several times, until you are quite sure that you have grasped the sense of it.

(*b*) Use your own words wherever possible. Do not attempt to write the paraphrase word for word, however: you should aim rather at expressing the sense and meaning of each part of the passage.

(*c*) Use simple, clear English, and break up any long and difficult sentences into shorter, more comprehensible ones.

(*d*) If you are faced by a complicated sentence construction in the original, you will nearly always find that you can break it down and understand it by doing a clause analysis.

(*e*) Do not change Person or Tense unnecessarily.

(*f*) Remember that your completed paraphrase should read fluently as a piece of continuous prose.

The short passage below is from *Richard II*, where the Gardener is instructing his two servants in their duties, and it is followed by a paraphrase which will give you an idea of what is required:

> Go, bind thou up yon dangling apricocks,
> Which, like unruly children, make their sire
> Stoop with oppression of their prodigal weight:
> Give some supportance to the bending twigs.
> Go thou, like an executioner,
> Cut off the heads of too fast growing sprays,
> That look too lofty in our commonwealth:
> All must be even in our government.
> You thus employ'd, I will go root away
> The noisome weeds, that without profit suck
> The soil's fertility from wholesome flowers.[1]

You go and tie up those apricots, which, like uncontrollable children, are making their father, the tree, bend under the load of their excessive weight. Prop up the bending branches. You, like an executioner, must cut off the heads of shoots which are growing too rapidly, and which appear too high in our garden-state. Everything under our control must be in proper proportion. While you are thus busy, I will go and pull up the harmful weeds which draw the goodness of the soil away from the sweet flowers.

[1] *Richard II*, III, iv, 29–39.

CONTEXT QUESTIONS

A context question, or 'gobbet', as it used to be called, is based on a few lines taken out of the text of the play:

> No more that thane of Cawdor shall deceive
> Our bosom interest:—go pronounce his present death,
> And with his former title greet Macbeth.[1]

To show your knowledge of the play, you are required to answer several questions on the context of the extract, and to do this satisfactorily, you must be able to recognise who spoke the words, and to whom, and under what circumstances they were spoken. You may fear that it will be very easy for the examiners to choose passages that you could not hope to recognise: in practice, however, if you have read the play carefully several times, and have only an average memory, you will find no difficulty in answering the questions—in fact, as you will see later, context questions provide an easy way of gaining marks, and can be completed more quickly, in the majority of cases, than essay questions.

Previously, candidates in an examination would expect to find context questions phrased in this way:

1. *Give the context of the following passages:*...

and in reply, taking the context given above as our example, they would write something like this:

These words were spoken by King Duncan to Ross, a Scottish noble, after Ross had brought him the good news that the King's generals, Macbeth and Banquo, had won a great victory. Duncan's kingdom had been threatened by a rebel named Macdonwald, whom Macbeth had killed in single combat, and by Sweno, king of Norway, who had been assisted by the treacherous thane of Cawdor. On hearing of Sweno's defeat, Duncan gives orders to Ross, in the words of the extract, to see that Cawdor is executed immediately, and his title given as a reward to Macbeth: 'What he hath lost noble Macbeth hath won.'[2]

[1] *Macbeth*, I, ii, 65–7.
[2] *Macbeth*, I, ii, 69.

In addition to this information, comments and explanations were expected on any difficult or unusual words or phrases in the passage.

The pattern of the context question has now changed; and although the questions are sometimes more searching, the answers are usually more economical of time. Here is a context question typical of those set by the West African School Certificate examiners:

Choose three of the following passages, and answer briefly the questions which follow:

1. (a)   *I blame you not for praising Caesar so;*
        But what compact mean you to have with us?
        Will you be prick'd in number of our friends;
        Or shall we on, and not depend on you?[1]

    (i) *Who spoke these words, and to whom?*

    (ii) *On what occasion were these words spoken?*

    (iii) *What answer was given by the person to whom these words were addressed?*

    (iv) *What had the speaker previously proposed should be done to the person spoken to, and who had dissuaded him, and by what argument?*

In reply, we might write:

    (i) These words were spoken by Cassius, to Antony.

    (ii) After Caesar's murder, Antony was at first afraid to approach the conspirators, but after receiving a promise from Brutus that he would not be harmed, he came to meet the conspirators, and it was then that Cassius addressed him in the words quoted.

    (iii) Antony replied that he was friends with them all, and loved them all, provided that they could give him reasons why Caesar was dangerous; and he asked leave to make Caesar's funeral oration.

    (iv) Cassius had previously suggested that Antony should fall with Caesar, but Brutus had dissuaded him, saying that their course would seem too bloody, and that Antony was only a limb of Caesar's, and not dangerous without his leader.

[1] *Julius Caesar*, III, i, 214–17.

57

Sometimes questions are asked to test your knowledge of unusual words or phrases in the context passage: for instance, in place of question (iii), this might have been asked:

What is the meaning in this passage of the word 'prick'd'?
Your answer would be:

(iii) 'Prick'd' means 'marked' or 'written'.

Another variation is to ask you to make a reference to some other part of the play: for example, here is an alternative to question (iv):

Mention another occasion in the play when people are found 'pricking' their friends and enemies.

You might answer:

(iv) After Brutus and Cassius have been expelled from Rome we find Antony, Octavius and Lepidus engaged in deciding which of their enemies should die: as Antony says:

'These many then shall die; their names are prick'd.'[1]

Do not be confused if the context is printed like this:
1 (a) *A. I have slept, my lord, already.*
    B. It was well done, and thou shalt sleep again;
    I will not hold thee long: if I do live,
    I will be good to thee.[2]
(i) *Who are A and B?*

Answer: 'A and B are Lucius and Brutus': or, better, 'A is Lucius and B is Brutus.' The latter answer leaves no doubt that you know exactly which is which.

To answer context questions well, you must have a thorough knowledge of the text and of the glossary, but extensive notes on words and phrases are not necessary; the purpose of a note is to help you to understand something that is not clear, and you should restrict your explanation accordingly. A useful method of preparation or revision for context questions is for two (or more) students to take it in turn to ask each other

[1] *Julius Caesar*, IV, i, 1. [2] *Julius Caesar*, IV, iii, 262–5.

questions modelled on those given as examples, on passages chosen at random from the text. If you feel that your knowledge of a particular scene or act is insufficient, confine your attention to that section until you have mastered it. When several students work together in this way, it is surprising how the weaker ones benefit, and also how soon familiarity with the text leads to a number of useful quotations fixing themselves in the memory.

The time factor is one which you must never neglect in examinations, and this applies especially to the answering of context questions, since, unless you are careful, you may find that you are wasting time by writing down more than has been asked for by the examiner. The only safeguard is to allow yourself a fixed time for each question, and not to exceed this. The only method of training yourself to say what you wish to say in this limited time is by practice. Select what is essential to the answer and discard the rest. It is better for an answer to be short than for you to penalise yourself unnecessarily by not answering all the questions. The specimen answer that you have been given is of average length.

Give variety to your work by introducing your answers differently when you can. For example:

'Orlando speaks these words to Rosalind.'

'Orlando is the speaker, and Rosalind the person to whom he is speaking.'

'After the wrestling, Orlando addresses Rosalind in the words quoted.'

Pupils frequently ask in which tense they should answer context questions. The safest method is to use the same tense for your answer as was used in the question. Sometimes examiners prefer the Simple Past Tense, and sometimes they use the Simple Present. The latter tense is used mainly, in conjunction with the Present Continuous Tense, to give an impression of reality, and to make you think that what you are reading is actually taking place: it is more dramatic.

If you can introduce a quotation into your answer, the answer is often made more effective, as you can see in the example given for the word 'prick'd'. Throughout the English Literature Paper, you must use quotations whenever possible, but they should always be appropriate, and never give the impression of having been brought in merely to show off your knowledge.

There is no need to copy out the words of the extract before you start to write your answer: it is a waste of time to do so. You must be careful, however, to number the answers correctly.

Finally, remember that to know one of Shakespeare's plays really well is no bar to your enjoyment of it. As your under-standing and knowledge grow, so will your appreciation and affection for the play, and the passages that remain in your memory will be a source of pleasure to you always.

CHARACTER STUDIES

Throughout our daily lives, we spend a great deal of time in consciously, or unconsciously, judging our fellows. We know, by instinct and experience, our friends, and those for whom we cannot feel affection; we know that A is lazy but generous, and that B is severe in manner but kind-hearted; D is boastful; C is timid. Those of us who live in schools see, every year, a number of new boys come into the school whose capabilities are unknown, and if we feel an interest in any one of them, we may try to find out something about him. The football captain, for instance, sees that a new boy, X, in his house, is tall and strong-looking, and thinks he might be a useful person for the football team, so he goes up to the boy, and asks him, directly, whether he can play football. The new boy answers that he is very good at the game. To help his own judgement, perhaps the football captain then asks a boy from the same village as X, whether X is really a good footballer. The second boy's reply depends, to some extent, on whether he is a friend of X or not. There is still doubt in the captain's mind, so to settle matters he arranges a trial game and puts X in the team. By X's performance, something will be learned about him— whether he is a good footballer, or whether he is an empty boaster.

To estimate characters in books or plays, we use methods similar to those employed by the football captain. First, we notice what the characters say about themselves; then we take into account what other people say about them; and, finally, we observe their actions. When the information so gained is added together, we are able to reach some conclusion, always bearing in mind the following points:

(*a*) *What the character says about himself.* Remember, that for some reason of his own, he may be trying to deceive people into thinking he is different from what he really is. Prince Henry, in *King Henry IV, Part II*, provides a good example of this tendency: for his own purposes, he pretends to be a careless, vain, and shallow youth, when really he is brave and determined. Or he may be a hypocrite, persuading people that he is good, when in reality he is planning wickedness, like Richard III. When, however, the character is by himself, we may assume that, in the speeches he makes, he is telling the truth; and it is in these solitary speeches, or *soliloquies*, as they are called, that we find the most trustworthy information.

(*b*) *What other people say about him.* While this may be a useful guide to a person's character, we must not forget that his friends may exaggerate his virtues, and his enemies magnify his bad points. We must try to take an unbiased view, remembering that sincere praise from an enemy is the highest praise of all.

(*c*) *His actions.* By observing whether his words and actions correspond, we can find out whether he is a hypocrite or a boaster; but one wrong action does not mean, necessarily, that a person's character is thoroughly or habitually bad: take into account the circumstances which may have forced him to act as he did.

The complete character is made up of many qualities, which we can call by several names—characteristics, traits, personal qualities, or idiosyncrasies.

COLLECTION OF MATERIAL FOR CHARACTER STUDIES, IN PREPARATION FOR EXAMINATIONS

Using the methods outlined in the previous section, students should be able to form an estimate of any character in a play: and it is far more interesting and useful to decide for yourself what a character is like than merely to memorise the comments of other people; but a warning is necessary. DO NOT EXPRESS OPINIONS WHICH YOU ARE UNABLE TO ILLUSTRATE OR SUBSTANTIATE BY QUOTATION OR REFERENCE FROM THE PLAY. Orlando may be brave; but to say so, without supporting your opinion, is not nearly so valuable as it would be if you added an illustration from *As You Like It* to prove your statement; all you need say would be that Orlando showed his bravery when he killed the lioness which was about to attack Oliver. When you gather information about the character you are studying, therefore, note, at the same time, any quotations or references which will help you to illustrate your point of view. Such quotations should not, normally, exceed four lines. Longer passages are not so easily memorised, and appear artificial when introduced into an essay. Your aim must always be to introduce quotations aptly and naturally, as though you were thinking in the language of the play.

Before you attempt to estimate the character of a person in a play, you must read through the entire play. Often, a character develops, or is modified, by events during the course of a play, and by the end may have given you an entirely different impression from the one you had at the beginning.

After you have completed your reading of the play, certain aspects of the character will be clearly in your mind: you have a picture of him. This picture may differ surprisingly from the one held by your friend, and it is most valuable for students to exchange views, each producing evidence from the play to support his opinion. By such interchange, you learn to look at a character from many different angles, and facts unperceived before are brought to light.

In the course of their work prior to an examination, students should collect material on all the important characters. This gives confidence: there is no haunting fear of being caught with nothing to say. A method is now described which has proved successful in accumulating facts, quotations and references in respect of any character it is desired to study.

On double pages in your notebook, or on a large sheet of paper, make five columns, and head them as shown below:

Name of Character	Characteristic	What he says (about) himself	What others say about him	His actions

The object now is to deal with each of the main characters separately, and for each of their characteristics or qualities, to note down at least one appropriate and illustrative quotation or reference, where this is possible, in each column. An example is given on p. 65, with Henry V as the character chosen.

More material than this could be gathered, but even the amount here set down is too great to be used in an essay of School Certificate length, where, supposing the size and speed of the candidate's handwriting to be average, about $1\frac{1}{2}$–$2\frac{1}{2}$ sides of foolscap would be sufficient. The important thing is that we have collected our material. All will not be remembered; but from the mass sufficient will remain for the student to have facts ready in his mind when he begins his examination.

Many of the Essay questions in the School Certificate paper are intended to test your understanding of character. The terms in which the questions are worded vary from the direct question on character, for example:

1. *Give a character sketch of Henry V*,

to the oblique, such as:

2. *'Every inch a king.' How far do you consider this quotation applicable to Henry V?*

or:

3. *With close reference to the play, account for your admiration and liking for King Henry V.*

Although only Question 1 asks directly for a character sketch or study, both the other questions are concerned mainly with Henry's character, though his characteristics are to be related to a particular aspect.

Let us imagine ourselves in the Examination Room: we have decided to answer Question 1.

FIRST. We must read the question through again, and make sure that we realise clearly what is being asked.

SECOND. We must make a plan for our essay. Nothing elaborate is necessary. Put down quickly the points you wish to include, and against them appropriate quotations or references. A convenient number of points is FIVE: each point will make about one paragraph. The Plan might look something like this (only material already collected being used for quotations):

Character Sketch of Henry V.

Leadership—Harfleur: Agincourt: 'O! 'Tis a gallant king': 'we band of brothers.'

Conscience and Piety—His regret for his father's usurpation: his care to have his attack on France justified: 'Praised be God, and not our strength, for it.'

Grim Relentlessness—Dislike of mockery (the Dauphin): Falstaff and Bardolph are cast off—'The king has kill'd his heart': the killing of the prisoners.

Name of character	Characteristic	What he says (about) himself	What others say about him	His actions
King Henry V	Leadership	'We few, we happy few, we band of brothers; For he to-day that sheds his blood with me Shall be my brother.' IV, iii, 61–3	'O! 'tis a gallant King.' (Fluellen) IV, vii, 11 The nobles all search anxiously through the camp for him when he has gone on his inspection on the eve of Agincourt (they are devoted to him).	Leads his men into the breach at Harfleur, and against great odds at Agincourt. Refuses to be ransomed: 'Come thou no more for ransom gentle herald: Thou shalt have none, I swear, but these my joints.' IV, iii, 122–3
	Piety	'Praised be God, and not our strength, for it!' IV, vii, 92	'The King is full of grace and fair regard.' (Canterbury) I, i, 22	Orders thanksgiving services to be said after Agincourt. Gets the Church to justify his claim to the French throne.
	Mercy and diplomacy	'Go you and enter Harfleur; there remain, And fortify it strongly 'gainst the French: Use mercy to them all.' III, iv, 52–4	'That's mercy, but too much security.' (Scroop) II, ii, 44	'When lenity and cruelty play for a kingdom, the gentler gamester is the soonest winner.' III, vi, 121–3 He points out the danger to be feared from Scotland.
	Humour	His wooing of Katharine.		The 'challenge' to Williams, and its sequel with Fluellen.
	Relentlessness, and dislike of mockery	'And tell the pleasant prince this mock of his Hath turn'd his balls to gun-stones.' I, ii, 281–2	'The King has kill'd his heart.' (Hostess) II, i, 91 'We would have all offenders so cut off.' (Henry, of Bardolph) III, vi, 116	Puts to death the conspirators (he allows them to sentence themselves—a grim joke). Orders all prisoners to be killed after the French have raided the baggage-train.
	Responsibility and conscience	'The slave, a member of the country's peace, Enjoys it; but in gross brain little wots What watch the King keeps to maintain the peace.' IV, i, 301–3 'Not to-day, O Lord! O! Not to-day, think not upon the fault My father made in compassing the crown.' IV, i, 312–14	Sir Thomas Erpingham indicates that he has no greater comforts than his men: 'Now lie I like a King.' IV, i, 17	Has reburied Richard's body and endowed chantries and paid alms-men, to atone for his father's sin.

Liking for a joke—His wooing of Katharine: his practical joke with Williams and Fluellen.

Mercy and Diplomacy—Caution lest Scots attack: Harfleur: 'when lenity and cruelty play for a kingdom, the gentler gamester is the soonest winner.'

To jot down some such plan need only take five minutes, and this time is not wasted. You have marshalled your facts, and in the resulting essay your ideas will follow a sequence, instead of being muddled together.

THIRD. Look over your plan, and see if you wish to change the order of any of your points, and then think for a few moments about your opening paragraph, which you wish to make effective.

FOURTH. Begin to write.

FIFTH. Read through your completed essay.

Something like this might result:

1. At the very beginning of the play, we learn from a conversation between the Archbishop of Canterbury and the Bishop of Ely, that King Henry V, in his youth, had led a wild and riotous life, but had reformed after his father's death, and become 'full of grace and fair regard'. The Archbishop is astounded at his learning and ability.

As we follow the career of the King, the reasons for Canterbury's admiration become clearer to us, for Henry is by nature a leader and a ruler. In his first interview with the French ambassadors, he speaks boldly and yet not boastfully, and is obviously supported by his nobles and by the Church. At Harfleur, urging his soldiers into the breach, there must have been few like Nym and Pistol, who were not stirred by his eloquence and eager to follow him; while at Agincourt, outnumbered five to one, his soldiers are determined to stay with him, although he offers a safe-conduct home to any who do not wish to fight. They are, indeed, a 'band of brothers', and Fluellen is their spokesman when he says: 'O! 'Tis a gallant king.'

Another notable quality of King Henry is his piety, which causes his conscience to be troubled at the memory of his father's usurpation of the throne. He has tried to atone for this. He is careful to make sure that the Church regards his attack on France as justifiable, and after the great victory of Agincourt we find him refusing to accept the credit for it:

'Praised be God, and not our strength, for it.'

Henry, as well as being brave and skilful in war, is a merciful man, and a clever statesman. The citizens of Harfleur are given every opportunity to surrender, and, on doing so, are used with mercy. This is not only humanity, but diplomacy: 'when lenity and cruelty play for a kingdom, the gentler gamester is the soonest winner.' It is Henry who shows his wisdom, also, by pointing out to his counsellors that danger is to be feared from Scotland while they are absent in France.

The King's nobility is not diminished by his sense of humour. In his conversation with Katharine, he shows himself a witty lover; and his practical joke of challenging Williams, and then giving the glove to Fluellen, for him to take up the challenge, and intervening before harm is done, shows that his humour is not spiteful; although the way in which he allows Scroop and the conspirators to condemn themselves could not be amusing to the sufferers.

Added to his many likeable characteristics, Henry at times reveals a grim relentlessness which is part of his strong nature. He does not like to be mocked, and the Dauphin's gift of tennis balls receives a severe reply. His old friend, Falstaff, is cast off —'The King has kill'd his heart', says the Hostess, when Falstaff is dying; while Bardolph, another companion of his youthful days, receives no mercy for his theft. The French prisoners are killed when their army does not behave according to the laws of war.

It must be admitted, however, that Henry's severity is usually merited; and our final impression of him is as a truly royal king who is loved by his people because he is also a man.

Notice, in the above:

(a) Our collected material has been used, though not all of it was necessary.

(b) The 'Five Points' have each been made into a paragraph, and short introductory and conclusory paragraphs have been added.

(c) The order of the points has been changed.

(d) Quotations are brought in naturally: where a quotation

is a complete line in the play, it is given a complete and separate line in the essay, but otherwise it is merged in the text.

(e) The length is about right for a full-scale School Certificate character sketch, though it could be shortened by about a quarter and still be long enough to obtain a good mark. An essay much shorter than three-quarters of the length of this one would be unlikely to gain a Credit mark.

A person's character, in real life, is not usually divisible into separate, clearly defined and describable characteristics; in most people, the good and bad are merged so that their frontiers are indistinguishable. Shakespeare's characters are similar; so it must be remembered that, although for examination purposes we may be forced to draw definite outlines, more lengthy and leisurely observation may reveal unperceived variation in them, just as the striking patches of colour on a butterfly's wing may prove, at a closer view, to be made up of subtle differences of texture and shade.

QUESTIONS ON PLOT

Many of the essay questions in the School Certificate Paper are designed to test your knowledge of the plot of the play you have been studying. The questions vary in type, and are sometimes combined with questions on character.

(a) *The Descriptive.* In such questions, you are required to give a simple description of a particular aspect of the plot, or to describe a scene in the play: for example,

1. *Give an account, with close reference to, and quotation from, the play, of the reasons for the quarrel between Bolingbroke and Mowbray, in* Richard II,

or

2. *Give a short description of the Garden Scene in* Richard II.

These questions are quite straightforward, and present no apparent problems, so that many candidates are tempted to hurry eagerly into writing their answers, without making a brief plan. This is unwise, as the chief danger in this type of question is that you will write too much, and by giving a detailed account, exceed the time which you should have allotted to that question. Never lose sight of the fact that the time factor is vital in examinations.

A question can easily be framed to test your knowledge of both plot and character:

3. *Describe briefly the first meeting between Macbeth and Banquo and the three witches, and say what you notice about the characters of (a) Macbeth, and (b) Banquo, from their speeches and behaviour in this scene.*

The same caution must be remembered: it will not be easy to keep your answer short.

(*b*) *The Narrative.* Here, you are required to trace the development of part of the plot, as in the question given below:

4. *Trace the steps by which Macbeth hoped to make his power in Scotland supreme, after the murder of Duncan, and show why he was unsuccessful.*

(*c*) *Dramatic Significance.* Comic Relief and Dramatic Irony have already been explained on pp. 35–8. Questions based on your understanding of these dramatic figures would be similar to these:

5. *Describe briefly the Porter Scene, from the beginning until the Porter opens the door, and explain the dramatic significance of the scene.*

In your answer to this, you would, of course, point out that comic relief is provided by the scene, and you would also show the irony in the Porter's pretence that he was keeper of Hell-gate.

6. *Give a short account of the scene immediately before Caesar's departure for the Capitol, and show, by reference and quotation, how Caesar's ignorance of what is planned against him is made to appear more tragic.*

Here is an opportunity to bring in any instances of dramatic irony that you can remember in this scene, to demonstrate that the use of this dramatic figure intensifies the tragic effect.

When the set book is a Comedy, questions are sometimes asked concerning the humour of certain scenes:

7. *Describe an incident or short scene in* As You Like It *which you find particularly amusing, and try to account for your enjoyment of it.*

At first sight, this question may appear very attractive. We all know what amuses us, so the choice of a scene is not difficult. The difficulty comes when we try to explain *why* we are amused, in a way that can be appreciated by the reader. It is safer, therefore, unless you have practised this type of answer, or are naturally very good at writing on humour, to avoid such questions.

EXAMINATION TECHNIQUE

It would not be realistic to lose sight of the fact that one of the important reasons for studying a Shakespeare play, as a set book, is to offer that book in the School Certificate Examination, with the earnest intention of doing well in the English Literature paper. The following hints are given with the object of helping candidates to make the most of their knowledge. Ignorance cannot be hidden in an examination, but knowledge can, by lack of method and technique in answering questions.

Preliminary points to remember are:

(a) *Answer all the questions you are instructed to do.* Unless it is otherwise stated on the question paper, the same number of marks will be given for each question. Supposing there are five questions, it is reasonable to assume that each will yield 20% of full marks: if you only attempt four questions, you are at once limiting the total it is possible for you to obtain to 80%. You must try, therefore, to do every question, even if the last one is shorter than the others.

(*b*) *Obey the instructions on the paper.* You will get no extra marks for doing more questions than you were asked to do. If a question reads EITHER (*a*)... OR (*b*)..., do only one of the alternatives.

(*c*) *Answer the question.* 'I know nothing of the life of Daniel', wrote a student in a Divinity examination, 'but here is a list of the Kings of Israel.' If you are in doubt whether you have sufficient facts to answer a question do not substitute what is irrelevant, as this student did. If you are uncertain of the meaning of a question, the remedy is the same as in the previous case—choose a different question.

IN THE EXAMINATION

1. When you are permitted to pick up your Question Paper in the Examination Room, the first thing to do is to read through all the sections in it which concern you, and to read them through slowly and calmly. Do this at least twice. Make sure that you understand the Examiner's instructions on the paper, and that you know how many questions to answer, and from which sections.

2. While reading through the paper, put a mark against any question which seems promising, and then consider each of these questions more carefully, and make your choice of the ones you intend to answer. If there is an optional context question, and you are able (as you should be) to recognise the requisite number of passages, then this must be one of the questions you answer. It is normally quicker and simpler to answer context questions than to write essays, and experience has proved that most pupils who omit the context questions put themselves at a disadvantage. If you are not good at essay writing, it is particularly important that you should make yourself good at answering contexts. Further advice about the choice of questions can be found in the Section dealing with Questions on Plot.

3. Calculate the time that you can allow for each question.

Subtract from the time available ten minutes, which you will require at the end, to read through your answers and make corrections, and to put your papers in order, and then divide the remaining time equally between the questions. *Conform strictly to this allowance.* Supposing that this works out at 20 minutes per question, use the first 5 minutes of that time to plan your answer, and the remaining 15 minutes for writing. If you write at average speed, 15 minutes is ample.

4. Number your answers correctly. An examiner's task is hard enough, without unnecessary confusion.

5. Try to write clearly. Set out your work neatly, and indent your paragraphs. A tidy, legible paper recommends itself at once.

6. Most teachers have their favourite methods of making corrections. The essential thing is that a correction or alteration should be clear, so if you have not learned a special way of correcting your work, when you make a mistake, cross the word out neatly with a single line, and ~~right~~ write the correct word next to it, or above it.

7. Pupils frequently ask whether they will be penalised for making a slight mistake, in word or punctuation, when quoting in an essay. Such an error is understandable, and unless it is very serious, is unlikely to cause loss of marks. The Examiner is not looking for opportunities to reduce your marks; he is eager to find something in your work for which he can reward you. The difficulty of punctuation of quotations is dealt with in the Section on Blank Verse, and the correct way of introducing and giving separate lines to quotations, in the Character Study of Henry V.

8. Finish writing 10 minutes before the end of the Examination, and read carefully through your answers, correcting neatly where necessary. Make sure that your written papers are in their proper order, with your name and number on each, and tie them together, if you are so instructed. If you write up to the very last minute of the examination, and then have

a frantic rush to put your papers together before the invigilator collects them, it is extremely likely that some foolish muddle, and possibly some serious errors in your work, will pass uncorrected to the examiner.

The Literature Paper of the School Certificate examination is lengthy, for it asks questions on a number of different books, and it can be quite unnerving for a candidate to turn hurriedly through the numerous pages in a seemingly vain search for the questions on the books he has prepared. So that the lay-out of the paper may be familiar, and candidates may have confidence in facing it, it is a wise precaution for teachers to pass round the class a copy of the paper for a previous year. Pupils then become accustomed to the size of it, and are not unduly worried if it takes them some time to locate the questions on their set books.

Some of the points mentioned here may seem unimportant, and some of the advice obvious. But every year mistakes *are* made, and it is to help *you* to avoid some of the unnecessary ones, that your careful attention to this Section is advised.

QUESTION PAPERS

The Question Papers which follow are included for use as tests of attainment, or as models for the teacher or pupil who wishes to compile further papers of similar type. The form of the questions, and their degree of difficulty, are comparable to those of the questions in the Shakespeare section of the English Literature Paper (Alternative I), of the Cambridge Oversea School Certificate (in West Africa, the West African School Certificate).

Questions have been set on the six plays which are most frequently chosen as set books.

The general instructions at the head of the first paper regarding time, and choice of questions, apply to the remaining papers also. The context questions have been made compulsory because, as was explained on p. 71, that is how they should normally be regarded.

General Instructions

There is an allowance of 5 minutes in which to read through the paper before you begin to write. This allowance is additional to the $1\frac{1}{2}$ hours given for the paper.

Answer Question 1 and TWO *other questions.*

Time—$1\frac{1}{2}$ *hours.*

MACBETH

1. Choose THREE of the passages (*a*)–(*d*), and answer briefly the questions which follow:

    (*a*) *Lady Macbeth*:   He that's coming
              Must be provided for; and you shall put
              This night's great business into my dispatch;
              Which shall to all our days and nights to come
              Give solely sovereign sway and masterdom.[1]

    (i) What plan does Lady Macbeth suggest later, to 'provide' for Duncan?

    (ii) What actual part does she play in the plan, and how does she correct a mistake made by her husband in it?

    (iii) For what reason does she not carry out the whole of the plan herself?

    (iv) Explain the Irony in the last two lines of this passage.

    (*b*)   This murderous shaft that's shot
              Hath not yet lighted, and our safest way
              Is to avoid the aim: therefore, to horse;
              And let us not be dainty of leave-taking,
              But shift away.[2]

    (i) Who speaks these words, and to whom?

    (ii) On what occasion are these words spoken?

    (iii) On whom does the speaker think the 'murderous shaft' may light, and where do he, and the person he is speaking to, go?

    (iv) What is the immediate effect of their departure?

      [1] I, iv, 67–71.   [2] II, iii, 148–52.

(c)   I will to-morrow—
        And betimes I will—to the weird sisters:
        More shall they speak; for now I am bent to know,
        By the worst means, the worst.[1]

(i) On what occasion does Macbeth speak the words of this passage?

(ii) When he next visits the weird sisters, what is he told?

(iii) What news does he receive immediately after his visit which makes it impossible to carry out a plan he had made?

(iv) Explain the meaning of the word 'betimes'.

(d)   Those he commands move only in command,
        Nothing in love; now does he feel his title
        Hang loose about him, like a giant's robe
        Upon a dwarfish thief.[2]

(i) Who speaks these words, and to whom?

(ii) On what occasion are these words spoken?

(iii) What effect does it have upon Macbeth's plan for fighting his enemies that those in his command are reluctant to help him?

(iv) Mention another occasion in the play when use is made, in a metaphor or a simile, of the words 'robes' or 'garments'.

2. Give an account of the arguments used by Lady Macbeth to persuade Macbeth to carry out the murder of Duncan. Which argument, do you think, was of most weight in influencing him?

3. EITHER (a) Give a short description of the Witches and their charms, and estimate how far their prophecies are responsible for Macbeth's final downfall.

OR (b) Describe the Banquet Scene, and explain, with reference to incidents in it, how it is a turning point in Macbeth's career.

4. By a brief examination of Macbeth's character, explain why you are, or are not, left with a feeling of pity for him at the end of the play.

[1] III, v, 132–5.   [2] V, ii, 19–22.

1. Choose THREE of the passages (a)–(d), and answer briefly the questions which follow:

   (a) These growing feathers pluck'd from Caesar's wing
      Will make him fly an ordinary pitch,
      Who else would soar above the view of men
      And keep us all in servile fearfulness.[1]

      (i) Who is the speaker of these words, and to whom is he speaking?
      (ii) On what occasion are these words spoken?
      (iii) Mention two things which the speaker orders to be done, in order to pluck 'growing feathers' from Caesar's wing.
      (iv) What punishment did the speaker receive later?

   (b) The taper burneth in your closet, sir.
      Searching the window for a flint, I found
      This paper, thus seal'd up; and I am sure
      It did not lie there when I went to bed.[2]

      (i) Who speaks these words, and to whom?
      (ii) What are the contents of the paper referred to in the third line?
      (iii) Who has put the paper there, and for what purpose?
      (iv) How does it, in fact, influence the person who reads it?

   (c) How foolish do your fears seem now, Calphurnia!
      I am ashamed I did yield to them.
      Give me my robe, for I will go:
      And look where Publius is come to fetch me.[3]

      (i) What fears did Calphurnia have, and what caused them?
      (ii) How did Caesar 'yield' to them?
      (iii) Who persuaded Caesar that Calphurnia's fears were foolish, and what arguments did he use to do so?
      (iv) Name one person who would have agreed with Calphurnia.

   (d) This is a slight unmeritable man,
      Meet to be sent on errands: is it fit,
      The three-fold world divided, he should stand
      One of the three to share it?[4]

[1] I, i, 76–9.   [2] II, i, 35–8.
[3] II, ii, 105–8.   [4] IV, i, 12–15.

(i) Who speaks these words, and to whom?

(ii) To whom is the speaker referring in these words?

(iii) What opinion does the person addressed in these words hold of the man whom the speaker considers 'unmeritable'?

(iv) On what errand has the 'slight unmeritable man' just been sent?

2. 'This was the noblest Roman of them all;
   All the conspirators save only he
   Did that they did in envy of great Caesar.'

With reference to incidents in the play, show whether you agree with Antony's estimate of the character of Brutus.

3. EITHER (a) Trace the mistakes made by the conspirators which brought about their final defeat.

OR (b) Give an account of the methods and arguments used by Antony to inflame the Roman citizens to turn against the conspirators.

4. With quotation from the play, give a character sketch of Julius Caesar.

RICHARD II

1. Choose THREE of the passages (a)–(d), and answer briefly the questions which follow:

(a) But, lords, we hear this fearful tempest sing,
    Yet seek no shelter to avoid the storm;
    We see the wind sit sore upon our sails,
    And yet we strike not, but securely perish.[1]

   (i) Who is the speaker, and to whom is he speaking?

   (ii) On what occasion are these words spoken?

   (iii) What has made the speaker so afraid for his position?

   (iv) What comforting news does the speaker give soon afterwards?

(b) It may be I will go with you: but yet I'll pause;
    For I am loath to break our country's laws.
    Nor friends nor foes, to me welcome you are:
    Things past redress are now with me past care.[2]

   (i) Who speaks these words, and to whom?

   (ii) On what occasion are these words spoken?

[1] II, i, 264–7.   [2] II, iv, 168–71.

(iii) Where is the person spoken to trying to persuade the speaker to accompany him?

(iv) What offer has the speaker just made?

(c)   *Gard.* Poor queen! so that thy state might be no worse,
I would my skill were subject to thy curse.
Here did she fall a tear; here, in this place,
I'll set a bank of rue, sour herb of grace;
Rue, even for ruth, here shortly shall be seen,
In the remembrance of a weeping queen.[1]

(i) What curse had the queen put upon the gardener's skill?

(ii) Why did she wish to curse his skill?

(iii) Where did the queen go, with her ladies, just before the gardener spoke these words?

(iv) Explain briefly the meaning of the last two lines of the context.

(d) *K. Rich.* That hand shall burn in never-quenching fire
That staggers thus my person. Exton, thy fierce hand
Hath with the king's blood stained the king's own land.
Mount, mount, my soul! thy seat is up on high,
Whilst my gross flesh sinks downward, here to die.[2]

(i) For what reason did Exton murder King Richard?

(ii) What were Exton's feelings after he had carried out the murder?

(iii) What reward did Exton receive from Bolingbroke for his action?

(iv) How did Bolingbroke promise to try to make amends for Richard's death?

2. Give an account of the causes of Richard's unpopularity with both nobles and commons.

3. Compare and contrast the characters of the King's noble uncles, John of Gaunt and the Duke of York.

4. EITHER (a) How far do you consider Bolingbroke was justified in his return to England?

OR (b) Give brief character sketches of TWO of the following:

(i) Aumerle.   (iii) Northumberland.
(ii) The Bishop of Carlisle.   (iv) The Queen.

[1] III, iv, 102–7.   [2] V, v, 109–13.

1. Choose THREE of the passages (*a*)–(*d*), and answer briefly the questions which follow:

(*a*) *Dauphin.* Say, if my father render fair return,
　　　　It is against my will; for I desire
　　　　Nothing but odds with England: to that end,
　　　　As matching to his youth and vanity,
　　　　I did present him with the Paris balls.[1]

　　(i) To whom is the Dauphin speaking in the words of the context?

　　(ii) On what occasion does he speak these words?

　　(iii) Mention briefly two occasions on which different people express views opposite to those of the Dauphin about Henry's youth and vanity.

　　(iv) What answer did Henry send in reply to the Dauphin's gift of tennis balls?

(*b*) We may as bootless spend our vain command
　　　Upon the enraged soldiers in their spoil
　　　As send precepts to the leviathan
　　　To come ashore.[2]

　　(i) Who speaks these words, and to whom?

　　(ii) On what occasion are these words spoken?

　　(iii) What reply does the speaker receive?

　　(iv) On receiving the reply, what orders does the speaker then give?

(*c*) *K. Hen.* Give me any gage of thine, and I will wear it in my bonnet: then, if ever thou darest acknowledge it, I will make it my quarrel.
Will. Here's my glove: give me another of thine.[3]

　　(i) What is meant here by the word 'gage'?

　　(ii) How is it that Williams has not recognised that the person speaking to him is the King?

　　(iii) Explain briefly the reason for the quarrel between Williams and the King.

　　(iv) How is the quarrel finally settled?

[1] II, iv, 127–31.　　　　[2] III, iii, 24–7.
[3] IV, i, 226–30.

(d) The sin upon my head, dread sovereign!
   For in the book of Numbers is it writ:
   'When the son dies, let the inheritance
   Descend unto the daughter.' Gracious lord,
   Stand for your own; unwind your bloody flag;
   Look back into your mighty ancestors.[1]

    (i) Who is the speaker, and on what occasion does he speak these words?

    (ii) Explain shortly why the speaker is anxious to persuade Henry to attack the French, and what inducement he offers.

    (iii) Which ancestor defeated the French particularly severely?

    (iv) What possible objection does Henry see to invading France?

2. EITHER (a) What part is played by the Chorus in *Henry V*?
OR (b) Explain briefly for what reasons Shakespeare brought Pistol, Nym, Bardolph and the Boy into the play, and say what was the fate of each.

3. With close reference to the play, show whether you would agree with the opinion that, from his drawing of the character of the King, Shakespeare had a great admiration for Henry V.

4. Write short character studies of TWO of the following:

    (a) Fluellen.   (d) Pistol.
    (b) The Dauphin.   (e) Katharine.
    (c) Exeter.

AS YOU LIKE IT

1. Choose THREE of the passages (a)–(d), and answer briefly the questions which follow:

(a) You will take little delight in it, I can tell you, there is such odds in the man: in pity of the challenger's youth I would fain dissuade him, but he will not be entreated. Speak to him, ladies; see if you can move him.[2]

    (i) Who is the speaker, and to whom is he speaking?

    (ii) On what occasion are these words spoken?

    (iii) Explain the meaning of the phrase 'there is such odds in the man'.

---

[1] I, ii, 97–102.   [2] I, ii, 170–4.

(iv) What causes the speaker later to turn against the challenger he mentions here?

(b) Thou seest we are not all alone unhappy:
This wide and universal theatre
Presents more woful pageants than the scene
Wherein we play in.[1]

(i) Who speaks these words, and to whom?

(ii) Where are these words spoken?

(iii) What 'woful pageant' has the speaker just seen, which makes him use these words?

(iv) Say in a few words how the person spoken to continues the metaphor of theatres and scenes in his next speech.

(c) There be some women, Silvius, had they mark'd him
In parcels as I did, would have gone near
To fall in love with him; but, for my part,
I love him not nor hate him not; and yet
Have more cause to hate him than to love him.[2]

(i) Who is the speaker, and on what occasion are these words spoken?

(ii) From the speaker's words, what mistake is it obvious she is making?

(iii) What reason has the speaker to hate the person referred to in the words of the context?

(iv) How does the speaker propose to revenge herself?

(d) A. Be of good cheer, youth. You a man! You lack a man's heart.

B. I do so, I confess it. Ah, sirrah! a body would think this was well counterfeited. I pray you, tell your brother how well I counterfeited. Heigh-ho![3]

(i) Who is A and who is B?

(ii) Explain the dramatic irony hidden in A's words.

(iii) What news has A just brought to B?

(iv) What has B been 'counterfeiting'?

2. Give a short account of the reasons for which (a) Orlando, (b) Rosalind and Celia, and (c) Oliver, made their way to the Forest of Arden.

---

[1] II, vii, 136–9.   [2] III, v, 124–8.
[3] IV, iii, 165–70.

3. EITHER (a) Explain the purpose of the Songs in *As You Like It*, and show whether you find them enjoyable or not.

OR (b) Compare and contrast life in the Forest of Arden, and life at the Court of Duke Frederick.

4. Give character sketches of TWO of the following:

(a) Adam.   (d) Phebe.
(b) Jaques.   (e) Oliver.
(c) Celia.

TWELFTH NIGHT

1. Choose THREE of the passages (a)–(d), and answer briefly the questions which follow:

(a)   Cesario,
Thou know'st no less but all; I have unclasp'd
To thee the book even of my secret soul:
Therefore, good youth, address thy gait unto her,
Be not denied access, stand at her doors,
And tell them, there thy fixed foot shall grow
Till thou have audience.[1]

(i) Who speaks these words, and on what occasion?
(ii) Who, in fact, is Cesario?
(iii) To whom is Cesario being sent, and for what purpose?
(iv) What is the result of his mission?

(b) I will drop in his way some obscure epistles of love; wherein, by the colour of his beard, the shape of his leg, the manner of his gait, the expressure of his eye, forehead, and complexion, he shall find himself most feelingly personated.[2]

(i) Who speaks these words, and to whom?
(ii) To whom is the speaker going to write the epistles referred to?
(iii) From whom are the letters supposed by the recipient to have come?
(iv) Say briefly what the result of the trick is.

(c)   My kind Antonio,
I can no other answer make but thanks,
And thanks, and ever thanks; and oft good turns

[1] I, iv, 12–18.   [2] II, iii, 171–6.

82

Are shuffled off with such uncurrent pay:
But, were my worth, as is my conscience, firm,
You should find better dealing.[1]

    (i) Who is the speaker of these words?

    (ii) Why is he so indebted to Antonio?

    (iii) Where does the speaker go, after he parts from Antonio?

    (iv) Why dare Antonio not accompany the speaker?

(*d*)   I prithee, gentle friend,
Let thy fair wisdom, not thy passion, sway
In this uncivil and unjust extent
Against thy peace. Go with me to my house,
And hear thou there how many fruitless pranks
This ruffian hath botch'd up, that thou thereby
May'st smile at this.[2]

    (i) Who is the speaker, and to whom are these words spoken?

    (ii) Who is the ruffian referred to in these words?

    (iii) What has happened to the ruffian?

    (iv) For whom does the speaker mistake the person spoken to?

2. What do you learn from this play about the duties and characteristics of the Clown?

3. EITHER (*a*) Discuss the view that Malvolio is too severely punished for his conceit.

OR (*b*) Do you consider that the plot of the play is easily credible, or do you think that there are too many unlikely incidents in it?

4. EITHER (*a*) Write a character sketch of Viola OR Sebastian OR Orsino.

OR (*b*) Explain whether you find the comedy scenes amusing, illustrating your answer by close reference to two of the scenes which you consider most effective.

[1] III, iii, 14–18.   [2] IV, i, 55–61.

A List of Shakespeare's Plays

We do not know the exact dates when each play was written or first acted, but we can be fairly certain of the general order, which is fixed by various kinds of evidence. Sometimes there is a written record of an early performance: for example, we have Sir Thomas Hoby's invitation to Sir Robert Cecil to attend a private showing of *Richard II*, dated 7 December 1595; and on 2 February 1602 (in our reckoning) a certain John Manningham, a lawyer, recorded in his diary that he had just seen *Twelfth Night*. Then there is Francis Meres, an Elizabethan critic, who in a book published in 1598 listed all Shakespeare's plays to date—not, unfortunately, in chronological order, but at least we know that those listed are earlier than 1598.[1]

Where there are no such positive records we rely on the more doubtful evidence provided in the plays themselves, by 'topical allusions' or by their style of writing. For example, the mysterious jokes of Macbeth's Porter about 'equivocation' almost certainly allude to a topic that was in everybody's mind in 1606—the state trial of a rebel (one of the 'Gunpowder' plotters) who admitted *equivocating* in his evidence. And as for style, we know that at the beginning of his career Shakespeare was writing English histories and romantic comedies, with plenty of rhyming verse, and that at the end of his life he preferred to write plays like *Winter's Tale* or *Tempest* that, beginning seriously or even tragically, have nevertheless a happy ending, and often employ a packed and involved kind of speech. Sometimes the evidence is conflicting. For instance,

[1] Meres's list includes a play called 'Love's Labour's *Won*'. Has this disappeared or have we here an alternative title for a play now known by some other name? And if so which? This is a famous puzzle.

parts of *All's Well That Ends Well* are in Shakespeare's earlier and simpler style, parts are in his latest manner. Perhaps then it is an early play, of which we have only a revised edition.

Probable date	Title of play	Evidence
1591–2	*Comedy of Errors*	Style
1592	*Henry VI, Parts 1, 2 and 3*	Records
1592–3	*Richard III*	Records
	King John (?)	
	Two Gentlemen of Verona	Style
1593	*Taming of the Shrew*	Style
	Love's Labour's Lost	Allusions
1594	*Titus Andronicus*	Records
1595	*Romeo and Juliet*	Style
	Midsummer Night's Dream	Allusions
	Richard II	Records
	Merchant of Venice	Allusions
1597	*Henry IV, Parts 1 and 2*	(Part 1 printed early 1598)
1598	*Merry Wives of Windsor*	Allusions
1599	*Much Ado About Nothing*	(Printed 1600)
	Henry V	Allusions— records 1600
	Julius Caesar	Records
1600	*As You Like It*	Records
	Troilus and Cressida	Records
1601	*Twelfth Night*	Records 1602
	Hamlet	Records 1602
1603	*Othello*	Records 1604
	Measure for Measure	Records 1604
1605	*All's Well That Ends Well*	Style
	King Lear	Records
1606	*Macbeth*	Allusions
1607	*Timon of Athens*	Style
	Antony and Cleopatra	Allusions— records 1608
1608	*Coriolanus*	Style
	Pericles	Records
1610	*Cymbeline*	Records
1611	*The Winter's Tale*	Records
1612	*The Tempest*	Records
1613	*Henry VIII*	Records

Reading List

This list provides the titles of a number of books connected with the study of Shakespeare's plays, for students who are interested in any special topic, or who wish to widen their knowledge and reading about Shakespeare, and his works and the age in which he lived. None of the books named should be so difficult, or expensive, as to make it unsuitable for the ordinary student. Where possible, the latest known price is given. Money can always be saved by buying second-hand books, and those books which were published years ago, and are consequently out of print, can, in fact, only be bought second hand. The student is advised to send his list of books required to a reputable English book-seller (any teacher will be able to provide a reliable address, or reference to the *Times Literary Supplement*, if this is possible, will supply some), and ask him to quote his prices. If these are acceptable, send postal orders, in payment, with your order.

If you have access to a school or city library, you may be able to borrow most of the books you require. If you are not able to do so, look up the topics that interest you in the Encyclopaedias in the reference section of the library, and you are sure to find some valuable information. In particular, the *Encyclopaedia Britannica* contains authoritative articles.

For a fuller and most useful Bibliography, you are referred to

Shakespeare—a Book List (National Book League; published by Cambridge University Press: 1s. 6d.).

All students should remember *that there is no substitute for a knowledge of the original text*. The examiner hopes to find individual judgements in your work, based on your study of the text, not ill-digested gobbets of information from well-known critics.

In this list, the following abbreviations are used:

C.U.P. Cambridge University Press
O.U.P. Oxford University Press
Ed. Edited by
Pub. Published by

ANNOTATED EDITIONS OF THE PLAYS, FOR SCHOOL USE

If the teacher wishes to help the class compile its own glossary and notes, and if expense is an important consideration, an edition with the minimum of footnotes is desirable, and a useful series is

The Plays (Dent: Kings' Treasuries edition: about 2s. 6d. per volume).

Students who are working without supervision, and teachers who do not specialise in English Literature, will require an edition with more comprehensive notes and glossary, which will be more expensive. Each of the following has its own particular virtues: the Pitt Press edition is perhaps the most comprehensive, but it might prove, at times, rather too detailed for the average pupil, and, unlike the other two editions mentioned, the notes must be referred to at the back of the book, instead of by the side of the text. The New Hudson Edition is comprehensive, without going into considerable detail about metre. The Oxford and Cambridge edition has very useful notes on the text, and on related topics such as character interpretation, dramatic significance, and Shakespeare's grammar, and would perhaps be most easily assimilated by oversea students.

The Plays (Pitt Press Shakespeare: ed. Verity: C.U.P.).
The Plays (New Hudson Shakespeare: ed. Hudson: Ginn and Co).

The Plays   (Oxford and Cambridge edn: ed. Wood: Gill and Sons).

The price of the first two editions detailed above is about 5*s*. per volume, and of the third about 4*s*., but they can be bought second hand for between 1*s*. 6*d*. and 2*s*. 6*d*. each.

SINGLE-VOLUME COLLECTED WORKS

A good edition for teachers and advanced students is:

The Works, Shakespeare Head Edition (Shakespeare Head Press and Blackwell, Oxford, 1947, 15*s*.).

This has clear type and large pages, and is a handsome book for a prize.

The Oxford edition is also a convenient edition for working with, and its text is substantially that of the First Folio, in modern spelling: its pages and type are smaller than those of the Shakespeare Head edition. All textual references in this book are based upon the Oxford Edition.

Craig, W. J. *The Works* (O.U.P. 1904, 12*s*. 6*d*.).

One of the recent, and best, editions, the text of which is used by some Examining Boards, is:

Alexander, P. *The Works* (Collins).

SHAKESPEARE'S LIFE AND BACKGROUND

A recent Life, which most students will find interesting, is

Brown, Ivor. *Shakespeare* (Collins, 1949, 12*s*. 6*d*.).

Drinkwater, J. *Shakespeare* (Great Lives Series, Duckworth, 1949, 5*s*.)

includes a useful study of the authorship controversies. Other books of general interest are listed below:

Harrison, G. B. *Introducing Shakespeare* (Pelican Books: Penguin Books, 1948, 2*s*.).

Lamborn, E. A. G. and Harrison, G. B. *Shakespeare: the Man and his Stage* (O.U.P. 1923, 5s.).

Williams, C. *A Short Life of Shakespeare* (O.U.P. 1933, 10s.).

Wilson, J. D. *Life in Shakespeare's England* (C.U.P. 1911 and Penguin Books, 1944, 2s.).

CRITICAL STUDIES OF THE PLAYS

These books are helpful for the stimulus provided by the ideas and opinions of famous critics on the plays.

Brooke, Stopford, *On Ten Plays of Shakespeare* (Constable, 1948, 10s.).

This contains analyses of *A Midsummer Night's Dream*, *Romeo and Juliet*, *Richard II*, *Richard III*, *The Merchant of Venice*, *As You Like It*, *Macbeth*, *Coriolanus*, *The Winter's Tale*, and *The Tempest*. The same author wrote

Ten More Plays of Shakespeare (Constable, 1932, 7s. 6d.)

in which he dealt with *Henry IV, Parts I and II*, *Henry V*, *Much Ado About Nothing*, *Twelfth Night*, *Julius Caesar*, *Hamlet*, *Measure for Measure*, *Othello*, *King Lear*, and *King John*.

Mackail, J. W. *The Approach to Shakespeare* (O.U.P. 1933) gives a valuable introduction to the plays.

Hazlitt, W. *Characters of Shakespeare's Plays* (1817)

can usually be found in a school library, but if a personal copy is required, Dent's Everyman's Library edition costs only 5s.

THEATRICAL PRODUCTION

Poel, W. *Shakespeare in the Theatre* (Sidgwick and Jackson, 1913, 2s. 6d.)

argues for a return to the Elizabethan methods of stage production.

Watkins, R. *Moonlight at the Globe* (Michael Joseph, 1949, 9s. 6d.)

describes how the author produced *A Midsummer Night's Dream* at Harrow School according to Elizabethan principles.

Webster, M. *Shakespeare Today* (Dent),

while interesting, may be more expensive.

SHAKESPEARE'S SOURCES

Carr, R. H. *Four Lives from North's Plutarch* (O.U.P. 1906).

This book reprints the complete lives of Coriolanus, Caesar, Brutus and Antonius, and shows how Shakespeare made use of this material.

Nicoll, A. and J. *Holinshed's Chronicle as used in Shakespeare's Plays* (Dent, Everyman Series, 1927).

AUTHORSHIP CONTROVERSY

For the Baconian Theories, see

'The Bacon-Shakespeare Theory' in *Encyclopaedia Britannica* (14th edition), xx, pp. 447–8.

No detailed list of books is given here, as most books on this topic are expensive, and unnecessary to the ordinary student.

GENERAL

The *Everyman Dictionary of Shakespeare Quotations* (Dent) is a useful companion for the serious student.

Other recommended school editions of the texts are:

The New Eversley Shakespeare, gen. ed. Guy Boas (Macmillan).

The Touchstone Shakespeare, ed. Guy Boas (Arnold).

The Warwick Shakespeare, ed. E. K. Chambers (Blackie).

The cost of book production is rising steadily, and prices given here may already be out of date. Be sure, therefore, to avoid disappointment, that you find out the current price for any book you wish to order, from the bookseller, before sending him money.

A Short Glossary

The words listed and explained here will frequently be met in your reading of the plays. Some of them will be unfamiliar only to oversea students, and are included for their particular assistance. Such words as 'thee', and 'yon', for example, are usually understood by English pupils, but may never have been met with by oversea students in their reading of modern English. Other words have changed in meaning since Shakespeare wrote, and those which often occur have been included to avoid confusion. The average annotated edition takes it for granted that most of the words given here will already be known to pupils, so this list is intended to supplement, and certainly not to supersede.

It is suggested that the best way to use this glossary is to commit it to memory. The irritation of having to refer to it constantly can then be avoided.

ADIEU, farewell, goodbye.
ANON, at once, immediately (often used to answer a call—Anon! = I am coming at once).

BRAVE, fine (in dress or appearance) 'O brave new world' (*Tempest*, V, i, 83).
BRAVERY, finery (in dress or appearance).
BUT, except, only.

CAN, be able; 'I can no more' (*Hamlet*, V, ii, 334)=I am able (to say) no more.
CLOWN, a country fellow (or a professional Fool).

DOFF, to take off clothes, etc. ⎱ contractions of 'do off' and
DON, to put on clothes, etc. ⎰ 'do on'.
DOTH, does.

E'EN, even
E'ER, ever.
ERE, before.

FOOL, dear, darling (may also refer to the professional Fool).

HAP, to happen, befall.
HAPPILY, perhaps, by chance.
HEAD, army, power (to make head = to collect an army).
HENCE, from here (hence! = be gone!).
HITHER, here, to this place.
HUSBANDRY, thrift, economy; 'borrowing dulls the edge of husbandry' (*Hamlet*, I, iii, 77).

LIEF, willing.
LIEGE, lord to whom loyalty has been promised.

MAKE, do; 'Now, sir! what make you here?' (*As You Like It*, I, i, 31).
METHOUGHT, I thought.
MINE, my; 'mine own servant' (*Antony and Cleopatra*, V, ii, 161).

NE'ER, never.
NICE, particular, scrupulous.
NOR...NOR..., neither...nor...; 'Nor time nor place Did then adhere' (*Macbeth*, I, vii, 51–2).

O'ER, over.
OFT, often; 'loan oft loses both itself and friend' (*Hamlet*, I, iii, 76).
OR...OR..., either...or...; 'Or Charles or something weaker masters thee' (*As You Like It*, I, ii, 277).

PERCHANCE, by chance, perhaps.
POWER, army, force.
prefix PER-, by.
PRITHEE, I beg, or pray, you; 'Prithee, go hence' (*Antony and Cleopatra*, V, ii, 171).

QUOTH, (he/she) says.
QUOTHA?, does he/she say?

SAW, saying, proverb; 'Full of wise saws' (*As You Like It*, III, ii, 156).
SOOTH, truth
suffix -EST, or -ST (for example, goest, wouldst), go, would (2nd pers. sing.).
suffix -ETH (for example, raineth), rains (3rd pers. sing.).
SUM, total, full amount.

THEE, you (2nd pers. sing.); 'I tell thee, churlish priest' (*Hamlet*, v, i, 262).
THENCE, from there.
THINE, your, yours (2nd pers. sing.).
THITHER, there, to that place.
THOU, you (2nd pers. sing.); 'Thou wouldst have mercy on me' (*Antony and Cleopatra*, v, ii, 174).
THY, your (2nd pers. sing.).

WHENCE, from where.
WHITHER, where, to which place.
WOT, know.
WOULD, wish (verb).

YON, that one over there.
YONDER, over there.

ZOUNDS, an oath, short for 'By God's wounds'.

You are advised, when making use of an annotated edition, not to worry too much about grammatical peculiarities, provided that you can understand the straightforward explanations of textual difficulties. You should, however, pay special attention to the explanations given in connection with allusions to proper names in the play, as questions are sometimes asked, in the context questions, on them.

INDEX

Figures in italic type indicate quotation from the plays

95

www.ingramcontent.com/pod-product-compliance
Ingram Content Group UK Ltd.
Pitfield, Milton Keynes, MK11 3LW, UK
UKHW042142280225
455719UK00001B/34